D0985674

Praise for *The Educator's Guide to Teaching Students With Autism Spectrum Disorders*

"Educator's will love this book. It is easy to follow and user friendly. It contains the basic principles of creating and supporting a quality learning environment for students with autism. The curriculum resources, assessment tools, and strategies are outstanding. It creates a clear vision of a successful program and guides you step by step on how to achieve that vision."

Mindy Stevens
Consultant to Schools and Families of Individuals
With Autism Spectrum Disorder
Center for Autism and Related Disabilities
University of South Florida
Tampa, FL

"This is a valuable book for many reasons. The content is comprehensive and user friendly, both for professionals and parents. The case studies are very realistic and show how collaboration occurs with related services. There are also excellent references given for further reading. I would highly recommend this book to anyone who is interested in learning more about autism spectrum disorders and the methodologies currently available."

Gloria Wolpert
Autism Program Director
Manhattan College
Bronx, NY

"*The Educator's Guide to Teaching Students With Autism Spectrum Disorders* offers educators and other stakeholders clearly articulated, effective practice options for students with autism-related disorders. This practitioner-friendly resource is an excellent resource for identifying, applying, and evaluating maximally effective interventions and treatments."

Richard L. Simpson
Professor of Special Education
University of Kansas
Lawrence, KS

"Ben-Arieh and Miller have combined their years of experience and expertise as educators of students with ASD and created an invaluable guidebook for teachers. *The Educator's Guide to Teaching Students With Autism Spectrum Disorders* is written in a very user-friendly style and will be an excellent resource for any teacher with a student with ASD in the classroom."

Terri Cooper Swanson
Assistant Professor
ASD Certificate Program Coordinator
Pittsburg State University
Olathe, KS

*To my husband, David, and to my children, Hila,
Idan, and Shanee, whose love and encouragement
sustained me throughout this project.
(Josefa Ben-Arieh)*

*To my husband, Forrest, and to my children, Elizabeth, Laura, and Noah.
Without their constant love and support this book would not have been possible.*

And

*In loving memory of my sister, Elizabeth M. Mackintosh (1939–1990),
who greatly loved and appreciated all children.
(Helen J. Miller)*

THE
EDUCATOR'S GUIDE TO
TEACHING STUDENTS WITH
Autism Spectrum Disorders

Josefa Ben-Arieh ▪ Helen J. Miller

CORWIN

A SAGE Company

Copyright © 2009 by Corwin

All rights reserved. When forms and sample documents are included, their use is authorized only by educators, local school sites, and/or noncommercial or nonprofit entities that have purchased the book. Except for that usage, no part of this book may be reproduced or utilized in any form or by any means, electronic or mechanical, including photocopying, recording, or by any information storage and retrieval system, without permission in writing from the publisher.

For information:

Corwin
A SAGE Company
2455 Teller Road
Thousand Oaks, California 91320
(800) 233-9936
Fax: (800) 417-2466
www.corwinpress.com

SAGE India Pvt. Ltd.
B 1/I 1 Mohan Cooperative
   Industrial Area
Mathura Road, New Delhi 110 044
India

SAGE Ltd.
1 Oliver's Yard
55 City Road
London EC1Y 1SP
United Kingdom

SAGE Asia-Pacific Pte. Ltd.
33 Pekin Street #02-01
Far East Square
Singapore 048763

Printed in the United States of America

Library of Congress Cataloging-in-Publication Data

Ben-Arieh, Josefa.
The educator's guide to teaching students with autism spectrum disorders/Josefa Ben-Arieh and Helen J. Miller.
       p. cm.
Includes bibliographical references and index.
ISBN 978-1-4129-5775-5 (cloth)
ISBN 978-1-4129-5776-2 (pbk.)
    1. Autistic children—Education. I. Miller, Helen J. (Helen Janet), 1949- II. Title. III. Series.

LC4717.B46 2009
371.94—dc22   2008049672

This book is printed on acid-free paper.

09   10   11   12   13   10   9   8   7   6   5   4   3   2   1

Acquisitions Editor:	David Chao
Editorial Assistant:	Brynn Saito
Production Editor:	Jane Haenel
Copy Editor:	Codi Bowman
Typesetter:	C&M Digitals (P) Ltd.
Proofreader:	Susan Schon
Indexer:	Molly Hall
Cover and Graphic Designer:	Scott Van Atta

Contents

Preface

This book is written specifically for every educator who teaches students with autism spectrum disorders (ASD). We have the greatest respect for you because we know the degree of dedication and enthusiasm necessary to make any real progress with these wonderful students. The fact that you have picked up this book suggests that you, like us, believe there is much more to learn about the education of students with ASD. So whether you are a general education teacher, special education teacher, speech-language pathologist, occupational therapist, physical therapist, social worker, or psychologist, our purpose is to help you, and your team, clarify a successful approach to working with a wide variety of children with autistic characteristics.

We were spurred on by our conviction that there are specific approaches that are more effective than others. Educators face many situations where best practices that are successful with other students do not bring the same expected results with students with ASD. So this book describes best practices for the ASD population; it focuses on approaches we have found successful in our work with individuals with this exceptionality.

Additionally, we believe that it is important to bring into the classroom the interventions that are based on the most recent research. We must all continually challenge ourselves to add to our repertoire of techniques; we must look for ways to promote independence, communication, and socially appropriate behavior along with academics in students who are often hard to motivate.

Finally, we were encouraged to write this book because we believe passionately in the potential of students with ASD. With well-chosen and intense intervention models, great progress can be made.

Acknowledgments

We owe a debt of gratitude to two of our students, Nicky and Karli, who many years ago started us both on the journey to learn about autism. This appreciation extends to all our wonderful students and their families who have taught us so much.

We are also indebted to our school districts and the dedicated professionals with whom we work, as well as to the many colleagues who have shared our passion for understanding the autism spectrum.

Our list of acknowledgments must, of course, include the many mentors, friends, and family members who, whether through words of support or by example, encouraged us throughout the years. We are truly grateful to each one of them for their positive influence on our lives.

We give a warm thank you to the Corwin staff and especially to David Chao, Brynn Saito, and Codi Bowman for their encouragement and clear guidance with this book.

An additional thanks to David Ben-Arieh for his help in preparing many of the figures and tables included in this book.

PUBLISHER'S ACKNOWLEGMENTS

Corwin gratefully acknowledges the contributions of the following individuals:

Rebecca S. Compton
Professor, Elementary Education
Director, Graduate Reading
   Program
College of Education
East Central University
Ada, OK

Sara Lynne Murrell
Fifth-Grade Teacher
National Board Certification—
   Middle Childhood Generalist
Greenville County Schools
Greenville, SC

Mindy Stevens
Consultant to Schools and
   Families of Individuals With
   Autism Spectrum Disorder
University of South Florida,
   Center for Autism and Related
   Disabilities
Tampa, FL

Gloria Wolpert
Autism Program Director
Manhattan College
Bronx, NY

About the Authors

Josefa Ben-Arieh earned her doctoral degree from the University of Kansas and worked as a postdoc at the Juniper Gardens Children's Project. Currently, she works as a consultant for schools helping teams create effective inclusive educational programs for students with autism spectrum disorders. Josefa also presents on various topics in autism at professional conferences and workshops nationally and internationally. In addition, she has authored and coauthored peer-reviewed articles, book chapters, and is the author of *How to Use Joint Action Routines* and coauthor of the book *Autism Spectrum Disorders: Interventions and Treatments for Children and Youth.*

Helen J. Miller, MA, CCC-SLP, is the autism coordinator in her school district. In this capacity she encourages research-based programming and provides training and consultation services to staff who work with students with autism spectrum disorder. Helen received a degree in Hispanic Studies from Edinburgh University, a master's degree in speech-language pathology from Kansas State University, and training in autism and education leadership from the University of Kansas. Her experience serving students with communication delays, including those with autism, covers a span of 20 years. She has presented on numerous autism related topics to university students, parents, and educators, and, as a Regional Autism Consultant for Kansas, Helen assists school teams across the state.

1

What Is an Autism Spectrum Disorder (ASD)?

Carla is a new first grader in Mrs. Edwards's class. Everyone is excited to get to know the new student. About a week after Carla joined her class, Mrs. Edwards starts to observe some behaviors that cause her concern: Carla can never get started on an assignment, she has frequent childish outbursts of anger at her peers, and she often seems to prefer the adults' company over that of her peers. Carla has been recently diagnosed with autism.

Autism was identified almost simultaneously both in the United States and in Europe. In 1943 in the United States, Dr. Kanner, a psychiatrist, is credited with first introducing the term *early infantile autism* in his article, "Autistic Disturbances of Affective Contact," where he described 11 students with unique characteristics that set them apart from others he had seen in his clinic. This article is considered pivotal, as it identified for the first time a separate category of mental disorder that was distinguishable from other mental disorders known at that time, such as mental retardation or schizophrenia. Coincidentally, during the same period, another physician was researching the same phenomenon on another continent—Europe. In 1944 in Austria, Hans Asperger described a similar set of characteristics in four boys with normal intelligence, which he called *autistic psychopathy*. Because these children had normal intelligence and language development, it was originally considered to be a type of higher functioning autism (HFA) and then later thought of as a separate disorder and labeled Asperger syndrome (AS).

In the latter part of the 20th century, based on Kanner's (1943) and Asperger's (1944) insightful observations, the similarities and differences in those with autistic characteristics were all finally recognized and described by the academic community as separate developmental disorders.

Prevalence and Prognosis

Various sources today report a dramatic increase in the autism prevalence in the general population such that it is believed that today autism is occurring at a rate of 6.7 in 1000 (Department of Health and Human Services Centers for Disease Control and Prevention [CDC], 2007). Furthermore, according to Individuals with Disabilities Education Act (IDEA) data published by United States Department of Education (DOE), from 1993 to 2006 there has been a 1,342% increase in the number of students aged 6–22 with ASD who have been served by IDEA (cited at *Fighting Autism*, n.d.; see Figure 1.1).

This statistic is further supported by the National Institutes of Health (NIH) which estimates that today approximately 400,000 people in the United States have autism, making it the third most common developmental disability (Morgan & Shoop, n.d.). The rise in the numbers of children diagnosed with ASD has led to an intense interest in the cause of the increase. Some speculate that better diagnosis of the condition, greater willingness to accept the diagnostic label, and a change in the social construct of autism are responsible for this upsurge while others believe it is due to environmental factors. Evidence continues to suggest that autism might have a strong genetic component. According to NIH (2004), at least 80% of the disorder is due to hereditary factors. In addition, an identical twin is more likely than a fraternal twin to have autism. Finally, studies on gender report that autism afflicts boys five times more than girls (National Research Council [NRC], 2001). Some researchers suggest that autism may be the result of a combination of factors such as a faulty immune system, metabolic disorders, viral agents, or some other combination of environmental hazards along with a genetic predisposition that triggers the disorder.

Figure 1.1   Number of Students With Autism—Percentage of Cumulative Growth

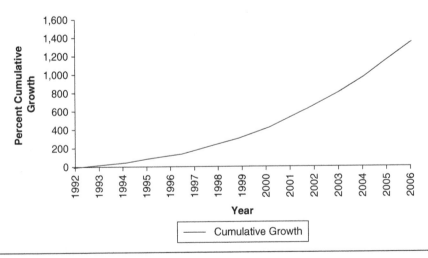

Source: www.ideadata.org and www.cdc.gov/nchs, retrieved March 20, 2008, from http://www.fightingautism.org/idea/autism.php. Data is based on the number of students served under IDEA in U.S. schools from 1992–2006.

Although autism is generally regarded as a lifelong disability, the variability and the severity of symptoms make it impossible to determine the progression of the disability over time. However, experts generally concur that IQ, language skills prior to the age of five, degree of disability, early intervention, the emergence of theory of mind, and the level of therapy available to individuals with autism are indicators of long-term prognosis (Happe, 1991; NRC, 2001; Simpson, Myles, & LaCava, 2008). Other predictors of long-term outcome include joint attention, symbolic play, and receptive language (Sigman, et al., 1999).

The prognosis for children in the spectrum becomes more encouraging than it was in the past. Today, with appropriate education, many are able to live with their families or in the community. In fact, many individuals with ASD perform well in jobs that require repetition and accuracy, although some may need mentors at the work location. When provided with intensive and appropriate early intervention, many students are then able to stay abreast of their peers in school and go on to complete high school programs or pursue advanced academic careers. Because the amount and the pace of progress are unique for each person, it is important for teachers to use research-based interventions that have been proven effective with many individuals on the spectrum. These interventions need, of course, to be tailored to the specific and unique needs of the student with whom you work.

Characteristics of Students With ASD

The *Diagnostic and Statistical Manual of Mental Disorders, Fourth Edition* (DSM-IV; American Psychiatric Association [APA], 2000) classifies autism as a subcategory of pervasive developmental disorders (PDD). In fact, PDD is viewed as an umbrella that encompasses Rett disorder, childhood disintegrative disorder (CDD), autistic disorder, pervasive developmental disorder not otherwise specified (PDD-NOS), and Asperger syndrome (AS) (Figure 1.2). The common thread to these exceptionalities is a pervasive impairment in several areas of development, such as social interaction skills, communication skills, the presence of stereotyped behavior, narrow interests, and an insistence on sameness.

PDD is generally viewed as a spectrum which, at the one extreme, includes individuals with normal to high IQ who may also have mild characteristics of autism to those at the other extreme who in addition to mental retardation may suffer from severe symptoms. One of the major factors contributing to the complexities of ASD is that each individual on this spectrum displays a unique combination of deficits and strengths, depending on the degree of the disability, cognitive ability, and comorbidity with other impairments. Other factors contributing to diversity in this population include each person's personality, interests, approach to solving problems, and learning styles (Janzen, 2003). Still, it is well documented that ASD results in abnormal functioning in several of the following areas: communication, socialization, behavior, cognition, and sensory integration. In the following paragraphs, we will describe the unique characteristics exhibited by individuals on the autism spectrum in each domain.

Figure 1.2   The Umbrella of Pervasive Developmental Disorders (PDD)

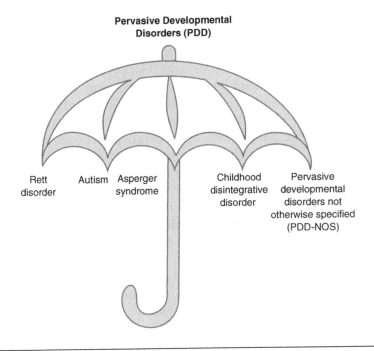

Communication

A predominant characteristic of ASD is a lack of understanding how we communicate with each other through turn taking with words and the nonverbal means, such as eye gaze, eye contact, and pointing. These deficits in joint attention may also be accompanied by profound delays in language acquisition. These skills can vary dramatically between students on the spectrum; the achievement of functional expressive language by the age of five years is considered one of the most important predictors of a positive outcome in autism. As with other characteristics, we can outline them on a continuum from most severe to least severe while remembering that anything that interferes with communication skills will have repercussions in many areas but particularly in that of social and academic functioning.

The most severe characteristics are

- no functional expressive language;
- no apparent understanding of language;
- lack of nonverbal communicative interactions (e.g., eye contact, eye gaze, distal point, turn taking with smiles and laughter);
- no response when name is called.

The less severe characteristics are

- language characterized by repetitiveness (e.g., asking the same question over and over again);

- echolalia—(a) immediate (e.g., responding with "what's your name?" when asked "what's your name?") or (b) delayed (e.g., reciting a conversation heard the day before);
- pronoun reversal (e.g., responding with "you want a drink" when the student actually means "I want a drink").

The least severe characteristics are

- difficulty in starting a conversation, maintaining a topic, or making what we call small talk;
- lack of awareness of some conversational conventions (e.g., maintaining eye contact, how close to stand to the person you talk to, speaking volume, and so forth);
- failure to understand figurative language and metaphors (e.g., "be careful not to step on somebody's toes");
- difficulty comprehending and expressing abstract concepts; limited by a concrete understanding of language;
- lack of reciprocity and not perceiving that the listener may have a different perspective.

The course of early language development is generally seen as one of the crucial elements that distinguish students with AS from those with autism. According to the *DSM-IV*, the language development of two- and three-year-olds with AS is typical, while those with autism have marked deficits and delays in language development before the age of three.

Remember: Students with ASD will take what you say literally, so if you ask them politely, "Are you ready to get started on your spelling?" they may well tell you, "No!"

Socialization

Many regard impairments in social competence as the core feature of this disability. As with the area of communication, the extent of the deficits in socialization varies greatly from student to student and correlates with the student's developmental level. Here are some of the characteristics common to students with ASD in the area of socialization.

The most severe characteristics are

- lack of social and emotional reciprocity;
- limited or abnormal facial expressions, body posture, eye contact, and other nonverbal forms of communication;
- not sharing an interest or enjoyment in objects, people, or events through facial expressions or by pointing them out to others;
- lack of play skills including turn taking and imaginative play.

The less severe characteristics are

- difficulty recognizing and responding to emotions, communicative gestures, and expressions;
- difficulty initiating and maintaining a conversation;
- difficulty intuitively tracking other people's beliefs and intentions during personal interactions;
- difficulty formulating and initiating questions to show interest in other people;
- difficulty interacting collaboratively in a group setting both in the classroom and during unstructured times (e.g., recess).

The least severe characteristics are

- difficulty with organization;
- difficulty in planning and prioritizing tasks;
- poor personal problem-solving skills.

These features seriously impede our students' ability to enter into and maintain peer and adult relationships. They also affect a student's ability to function appropriately in the school environment.

Remember: Not all students with ASD display all these characteristics.

Behavior

Another area greatly impacted by ASD is behavior. Expect students to display some of the following characteristics:

- Preference for solitude
- Preference for sameness and difficulty with changes of any sort
- Inflexible insistence on nonfunctional routines or rituals
- Use of objects in an unconventional way (e.g., spinning a car's wheels over and over again)
- Preoccupation with one or more stereotyped and restricted topics of interest (e.g., an intense interest in trains)
- Inability to participate in pretend games
- Stereotyped and repetitive motor movements (e.g., hand or finger flapping)
- Severe tantrums which might include aggressive or self-injurious behaviors (e.g., biting one's self or others and head banging)
- Excessive concern with doing the right thing
- Socially unacceptable behaviors (e.g., nose picking)
- Delays in the development of age-appropriate adaptive behavior self-help skills (e.g., dressing, toileting, grooming, and so forth)

In conclusion, the behavior of individuals with autism is marked by both excesses and deficits that greatly interfere with their ability to function in their environment and to effectively benefit from interactions with the social world around them.

Remember: Behaviors fulfill a communicative function for the student. Therefore our goal is never to simply eliminate an inappropriate behavior but to replace it with another more socially appropriate one.

Cognition

In the cognition area, students with ASD display unique features that impact how they process new information. These characteristics may include the following:

- Uneven repertoire of skills (splinter skills), such as, a special facility for calculating math facts but lack of comprehension of simple stories.
- An ability to focus on a seemingly trivial or irrelevant item of interest (stimulus overselectivity) while displaying an extremely short attention span for topics of less interest.
- May have a short attention span for topics of little interest while hyperfocusing on topics of high interest and thus often lose track of time.
- Diminished motivation to learn new material. (Often our students are not reinforced by social praise or tangible items used with typically developing peers, such as stickers.)
- Generalization difficulties. (Students with ASD tend to either overgeneralize or undergeneralize concepts. A student, for example, can learn to match the word *pen* with the relevant object in a classroom but fail to generalize the word to *pens* they see in other places.)
- Difficulties processing multiple cues at the same time (e.g., a verbal message, voice intonation, and facial expression).

Remember: Awareness of the unique cognitive difficulties your student has will help you devise strategies to overcome them.

These characteristics make integrating students with ASD in the general curriculum particularly challenging. Fortunately, many strategies have already been developed, and they are discussed in Chapter 5.

Sensory

It has been well documented that students with ASD struggle with sensory processing issues to various degrees (Anzalone & Williamson, 2000; Dunn, 2008) and can experience either oversensitivity or undersensitivity in one or more of the sensory modalities—visual, tactile, auditory, olfactory, vestibular (the system found in the inner ear that is responsible for balance and movement), and proprioceptive (the system responsible for providing the nervous system with information about the location of a body part through movements of muscles and joints) domains. Some abnormal sensory stimulation issues experienced by our students with ASD include the following:

- Sensitivity to touch that cause a student to wear only certain types of clothing, to refuse to eat a certain food because of its texture, or to react strongly to a light touch on his shoulder
- Sensitivity to odors that cause a student to react negatively to smells from the cafeteria or the smell of shampoo or lotion used by teachers or peers
- Lack of responsiveness to specific sounds and oversensitivity to others of a certain pitch
- Sensitivity to the hum and flicker of florescent lighting
- Insensitivity to pain
- Hyperarousal or hypoarousal
- Difficulty with activities that require eye-hand coordination
- Clumsiness and unusual posture
- Toe walking
- Self-stimulating behaviors, such as rocking or flicking fingers in front of the eyes

Remember: It is helpful to keep in mind that some inappropriate behaviors can be triggered by abnormal sensory processing difficulties.

In conclusion, it is important to realize that our students' sensory needs might prevent them from functioning appropriately in their environment. Ideas for treatment and interventions are discussed in Chapter 5.

The description of autism provided in this chapter was not meant to be exhaustive but to provide you with basic information of this intriguing exceptionality and, consequently, to help you understand the interventions suggested in the following chapters. Remember our student Carla described in the vignette at the beginning of the chapter? Thanks to Mrs. Edwards's understanding of autism, she was able to implement some interventions that have helped Carla cope better in her class. In the next chapters, we will share with you these strategies that we have also found extremely helpful for our students.

2

Assessment

John's mom and dad struggle to understand why their child, who seems so very bright in many ways, has such a hard time socially and academically. Family life seems to be one endless battle. Despite their thoughtfulness, they walk on eggshells around their son. Although diagnosed with attention deficit hyperactivity disorder (ADHD) and on medication, which has helped a little, there are still many areas in which he acts so differently from his friends and siblings. They feel there must be another answer, and so they begin their search. The first step they take is to ask for an evaluation of their son by both their family doctor and by the special education department at their son's school.

Is the situation described in this vignette familiar to you? Have you seen these kids struggle with school issues as well, such as not handing in homework on time, losing papers, not following directions, or getting into arguments with peers or teachers? What did the staff in your school recommend these parents do? This chapter will first address some issues that would need to be considered when administering various assessment tools for students on the autism spectrum. We will then offer a brief description of the various areas to be assessed and commonly used tools.

Assessment Issues

School staff is often the first to recognize that a student experiences significant difficulties academically, behaviorally, and socially. However, you, as an educator, may be quite reluctant to share such concerns fearing that the family might not be ready to hear that their child is different from his or her peers. In addition, you are well aware that they might both fear and resent the stigmatization that is attached to a label.

Furthermore, conducting an assessment is often time-consuming and expensive. Thus, before embarking on an evaluation, school staff must seriously consider how broad the evaluation should be and how beneficial it will be to the student and to the school. The questions we might ask relate to whether the proposed assessment will lead to better interventions or help answer questions parents and school staff might have, and whether it will help a student's physician make a better diagnosis or help the student better understand his or her challenges?

There are other questions to consider as well that are related to the reliability of an assessment: How reliable are the instruments that are being used and how well do they reflect the abilities of a specific student? Should standardized testing be used or are nonstandardized tests better tools for use with individuals with autism spectrum disorder (ASD)? Who is authorized to administer a test, and once the results are obtained, how can they benefit the school staff?

When considering the results of an assessment, we must remember that they all have limitations, and consequently, our conclusions should be drawn cautiously and judiciously. Assessments might be affected by factors such as the physical setting in which they take place (e.g., lighting and temperature), the physical comfort of the person that is being assessed (e.g., hunger and thirst), and the skill of the person administering the test. In addition to these general issues, there are other concerns specific to the assessment of individuals with autism. For instance, because of these students' language impairments, the commonly used tools for assessing IQ, such as the Wechsler intelligence scales (Wechsler, 1997, 2002, 2003) might fail to accurately measure the intelligence of a student with ASD. Additionally, behaviors exhibited by this population, including their lack of motivation, distractibility, and resistance to change in routine, often interfere with testers' ability to obtain an accurate picture of an individual's capabilities. The challenge of conducting an appropriate assessment for individuals with autism is augmented, in particular, by the multifaceted and interwoven range of deficits and excesses exhibited by individuals with autism in all areas of development: communication, socialization, behavior, academics, physical, and sensory (Wetherby, Prizant, & Schuler, 2000).

Remember: At best, tests only tell us a current level of a student's performance; they don't tell us how much the student will ultimately achieve.

Generally, from a school perspective, there are two main reasons for conducting an assessment for a student: (a) establishing eligibility for special education services, and (b) determining the strengths and deficits to be addressed in an individualized educational plan (IEP). The Individuals with Disabilities Educational Act (IDEA) requires the school to conduct a comprehensive evaluation to qualify students, even those as young as three years old, for services. There are, in fact, two kinds of assessments that can meet this requirement: an educational one and a clinical one.

Educational Assessment

An educational assessment is conducted by school personnel and by a multidisciplinary team that typically includes a psychologist, occupational therapist (OT), physical therapist (PT), speech-language pathologist (SLP), special education teacher, and, if available, an autism specialist. Each of these professionals gathers information specific to their developmental domain—overall intelligence, behavioral characteristics, fine and gross motor abilities, communication and social skills, present academic levels of functioning, and other traits unique to the student. The purpose of such an assessment will be as follows:

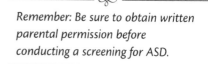

Remember: Be sure to obtain written parental permission before conducting a screening for ASD.

- Establish the student's eligibility for services
- Provide an estimate of a student's present levels of functioning
- Target areas for intervention

Clinical Assessment

In addition to, or prior to, the school's assessment, many families independently seek an evaluation either from a local psychologist or psychiatrist or from a multidisciplinary team at a regional health care center. A medical evaluation will assess both the developmental level and biomedical issues. Children are frequently referred for further testing such as genetic and allergy assessments.

The following section will describe in more detail the assessment tools that are commonly used for the evaluation of individuals with ASD.

Remember: Testing is not an exact science; therefore, we are looking for a preponderance of evidence to confirm or rule out the diagnosis of ASD.

Diagnosis and the Assessment Process

As parents search for answers, the professionals they contact are required to sort out many aspects of behavior to first correctly diagnose and then accurately describe the strengths and weaknesses of the child. Because of the complexity and pervasive nature of ASD (National Research Council [NRC], 2001), an interdisciplinary team approach is highly recommended. This comprehensive evaluation may draw from the expertise of many professionals—educational and developmental specialists, OTs, PTs, SLPs, and pediatric neurologists, as well as child psychiatrists and psychologists—to address all the areas of student development. As a member of a school team, you may be asked to participate from the very beginning as part of a diagnostic team, or you may be brought in afterwards to assist with further assessment.

The diagnostic and assessment process will usually start with direct observation of the student. Typically, observations are done either as the initial step in directing the course of further assessment or as the mainstay of the evaluation process. If your school has an autism specialist, this person would conduct an observation and may be assisted by the special education teacher and the school psychologist. Observations should be conducted over at least a couple of days and during a variety of activities, such as during physical education (PE), music, recess, lunch, and academics. The times and places of the observations should be guided by the regular education teachers who have been able to observe where and when the student's behavior most differs from his or her peers.

After completing the observation, the following areas are usually addressed in a comprehensive evaluation and assessment process:

- Medical and developmental history
- Psychological and behavioral assessment
- Academic assessment
- Communication and social assessment
- Occupational and physical assessment
- Sensory assessment
- Neuropsychiatric assessment (when medical professionals participate)

It is crucial to begin this evaluation with as much input from the family as possible and to provide the families with support and guidance throughout these early stages of assessment and diagnosis (Prelock, Beatson, Bitner, Broder, & Ducker, 2003). The parents of students with autism are usually troubled by their student's behavior and, when approached in a positive and accepting manner, are eager to engage in the process of discovering what causes their child's difficulties. Because for many families the label of autism is frightening, professionals must proceed with care and compassion, involving families as early in the process as possible. Furthermore, the medical and developmental history that they provide is an important first step in the process of determining whether their child might qualify for a diagnosis of Asperger syndrome (AS) or autism. For example, according to the *Diagnostic and Statistical Manual of Mental Disorders, Fourth Edition (DSM-IV)*, one of the distinguishing factors between autism and AS is on the basis of the student's language development. The language development of students with AS tends to be typical except for the pragmatic or social communication function and the acquisition of more abstract language; students with autism, regardless of cognitive level, have delayed language development and are often referred for speech-language evaluation and intervention by three years of age.

The medical and developmental assessment should include

- family history—especially a description of members who have had neurological disorders,

- pregnancy and neonatal development,
- physical assessment,
- early childhood development,
- leisure activities including play skills, and
- communication and social development.

Once gathered, this medical and developmental history will provide direction for all members of the assessment team as they proceed with their evaluation of the student.

Psychological and Behavioral Assessment

One of the first steps in assessment is the administration of screening instruments, which can serve to encourage consideration of the many characteristics of ASD. They should be filled out by the parents and the teachers who know the student best under the guidance of someone who specializes in the field. A listing and description of some of these screening instruments that are currently used are provided in Resource A.

Next, students with ASD need to be assessed for their intellectual functioning by a psychologist. Keep in mind the important role that cognitive ability plays in both diagnosis and in educational planning: Those with AS typically have average to above-average ability, and those with autism can range from severely deficient to superior intellect. At the same time, it is important to consider the behavioral and adaptive functioning level of the student (i.e., how the student uses his or her potential to adapt to environmental demands) because these may be significantly impacted in those with ASD. Even students with average cognitive ability may show deficits in adaptive behavior that interfere with their achieving independence. The psychologist will also determine the presence of restricted patterns of behavior, interests, and activities, and the developmental appropriateness of these interests and activities. Some of the more common tools used by psychologists are also included in Resource A.

Academic Assessment

A comprehensive evaluation of a student will include a battery of tests such as *The Woodcock-Johnson III Tests of Achievement* (WJ III) (Woodcock, McGrew, & Mather, 2001) to determine academic functioning level. For students with whom you cannot use standard tests there are a number of other tools to determine the level of performance and in helping you to identify educational objectives for a student with autism, such as

Remember: Students on the spectrum have splinter skills.

The Psychoeducational Profile, Third Edition (PEP-3) (Schopler, Lansing, Reichler, & Marcus, 2005) and *The Assessment of Basic Language and Learning*

Skills-R (ABLLS-R) (Partington, 2006). These tests, typically administered by the special education teacher, may take well over an hour to complete, depending on the student's level of cooperation. The information obtained, though, can help professionals develop effective IEPs as well as track a student's progress in the acquisition of skills in all areas of development: academics, social interaction, communication, behavior, and self-help skills. These instruments and others are also described in Resource A.

Communication and Social Assessment

Because one of the core deficits of ASD is in the area of communication, a complete speech and language evaluation is imperative. An SLP will want to assess not only the receptive and expressive language abilities of the student but most specifically the social aspect or pragmatics of language use (Woods & Wetherby, 2003). Assessment of both the speech (articulation/phonological) skills and the formal language skills, such as the ability to understand and use the vocabulary and grammatical structures of the language, may even reveal average or above-average ability. However, assessment of other aspects of communication is likely to reveal the core difficulties faced by students with ASD. Some of these stumbling blocks are especially noticeable in reading comprehension tasks, such as making inferences, responding to both simple and complex questions, and understanding the meaning of the whole as opposed to understanding discrete elements. In the area of pragmatics, the social use of language, the SLP will check a student's conversational skills, including responding appropriately to verbal and nonverbal cues from the conversational partner. The student's use of nonverbal communication, such as point, gesture, referencing, and eye-gaze, will also be considered along with the prosody of speech (e.g., volume, stress, and pitch). And finally, the SLP will analyze the student's comprehension of abstract language, such as idioms, and his or her knowledge of when others are joking or teasing.

An assessment of a student's sociocommunicative level must also include information on how he or she performs in a group as compared to one-on-one, how the student interacts with peers at lunchtime and out on the playground, and whether or not he or she is developing play and friendship skills. Helpful tools for identifying the strengths and deficits of students with ASD in the area of communication and social development are delineated in Resource A.

Finally, the team must consider whether the student's theory of mind (ToM) development is age appropriate. ToM refers to an understanding that people can have different thoughts from each other about the same set of circumstances and that we can even think about our thoughts and those of others. Table 2.1 is a chart describing the typical development of ToM.

Here is a short description of some of the various tests that one can perform to check the level of the ToM development for a student with ASD:

Table 2.1   Typical Development of Theory of Mind (ToM)

Age	ToM Tests	Skill
1- to 2-year-old		Joint attention Social referencing
3.5- to 5-year-old	1. First order of ToM (Sally-Anne Scenario)	"She knows that . . ." "She thinks that . . ." "She wants . . ."
	2. Mental-physical distinction	Thinking about a dog/holding a dog (which one character can stroke the dog?)
	3. The function of the brain	Lack of realization that the brain has both physical and mental functions (dreaming, wanting, thinking, keeping secrets . . .)
	4. Distinguishing between appearance and reality	A candle fashioned in the shape of an apple—the object is an apple (errors in realism)
	5. Seeing-leads-to-knowing tests (penny hiding game)	Understanding where knowledge comes from/who knows what/who doesn't know what (deception)
	6. Inferring from gaze direction when a person is thinking or what a person might want	Understanding what a certain gaze direction means (interest in objects, thinking about something)
	7. Monitoring one's own intentions (shooting a toy gun at targets)	Ability to differentiate between intention and actual outcome (correctly answering the question, "Which target did you mean to hit?")
6- to 7- year-old	1. Second order of ToM (the ice-cream man)	"She thinks (knows) that he thinks that . . ."
	2. Understanding that emotions can also be caused by mental states such as desires and beliefs	You can be happy also because you *think* you are getting what you wanted
	3. Understanding white lies	Understanding that you might thank someone for a gift you do not like to avoid hurting his or her feelings
7-year-old to adolescence	Higher order of ToM	Understanding faux pas, irony, humor, sarcasm, and nonverbal body language

1. *Sally-Anne Scenario* (Baron-Cohen, Leslie, & Frith, 1985)

   The teacher tells the student a story about two girls: Sally and Anne. Sally has a basket. Anne has a bag. Sally puts a candy in her basket, while Anne looks on. Then Sally goes out for a walk. While Sally is gone, Anne takes the candy out of Sally's basket and puts it into her bag. Now Sally comes back and she wants to eat her candy.

   The question the teacher asks her student now is, "Where will Sally look for her candy? Why?"

   Correct response: Sally will look for her candy in her basket because that's where she put it. It means that the student has passed the first order of ToM; that is, the student understands that another person might have other thoughts about an item than he or she does.

2. *The Ice Cream Story* (Baron-Cohen, 1989)

   This is a story about John and Mary. They live in this village. Right now they are playing in the park. Along comes the ice cream man. John would like to buy an ice cream but he has left his money at home. He is very sad. "Don't worry," says the ice-cream man, "you can go home and get your money and buy some ice cream later. I'll be here in the park all afternoon." "Oh good," says John, "I'll be back in the afternoon to buy an ice cream." So John goes home. After John has left, the ice cream man changes his mind and tells Mary that he wants to drive his van to the church to see if he can sell any ice cream outside there. The ice cream man drives over to the church. On his way he passes John's house. John sees him and says, "Where are you going?" The ice cream man says, "I'm going to sell some ice cream outside the church." So off he drives to the church. Now Mary goes home, and later she goes to John's house. She knocks on the door and asks, "Is John in?" "No," says his mother, "he's gone out to buy ice cream."

   The teacher's question is, "Where does Mary think John has gone to buy an ice cream and why?"

   Correct response: Mary thinks that John has gone to buy ice cream in the park because that's the location Mary heard the ice cream man tell John that he was going to sell ice cream the last time she saw them talking. This means that the student has passed the second order of ToM; that is, he or she understands that one person has thoughts about another person's thoughts regarding an object.

3. *The Penny Hiding Game* (Baron-Cohen, 1992; Baron-Cohen, & Goodhart, 1994)

   Give a student a penny and ask him or her to hide it in one of his or her palms so that you have to guess in which palm it is hidden.

   Correct response: The student hides his or her hands behind his or her back to perform this task. This means that the student understands deception. He also understands that people learn from seeing, and therefore, it is necessary to hide the hands behind one's back.

Other tests include:

4. *Reading the Mind in the Eyes* (Baron-Cohen, 2001)

5. *An Informal Test of Social Know-How* (Dewey, 1998)

6. *Strange Stories* (Happe, 1994)

7. *A New Test of Social Sensitivity: Detection of Faux Pas in Normal Children and Children With Asperger Syndrome* (Baron-Cohen, O'Riordan, Stone, Jones, & Plaisted, 1999)

Motor Skills and Physical Assessment

Students with ASD may have fine and gross motor delays. An OT will be able to analyze the different aspects of fine motor development, such as handedness, pincer grasp, eye-hand coordination, all of which affect daily living skills, such as writing, utensil use, dressing, and playing with small manipulatives. The PT will analyze the student's gross motor development. Students with ASD may be very agile and coordinated, or they may have significant difficulties or differences related to motor movements, such as toe walking, body posture, and muscle tone. Both the OT and the PT will assess the coordination and motor planning deficits evident in some students with ASD.

Sensory Assessment

Students with ASD are likely to experience various degrees of difficulty processing the information that comes to them through the five senses (vision, hearing, smell, taste, and touch) as well as the vestibular and proprioceptive systems. They may be hypersensitive or hyposensitive to the stimuli around them, and among other things, they may struggle with motor planning for both gross and fine motor activities and self-regulation. Because these challenges deeply affect these students' ability to interpret and cope with their environment and with their internal states, a systematic analysis of their sensory integration ability is a vital part of any comprehensive evaluation. Several evaluation tools, such as *The Sensory Profile* (Dunn, 1999), are available to assist in this assessment (see Resource A).

Neuropsychiatric Assessment

A psychiatrist's expertise is needed to determine the extent to which some behaviors are caused by underlying specific psychiatric disorders, such as compulsions, obsessions, depression, or anxiety. These may overwhelm a student and may require medication to alleviate their symptoms. Because research indicates that ASD runs in families, genetic testing is sometimes recommended. Additionally, seizures are prevalent in students with ASD (20% to 35% of students), and this will

Remember: In many areas, assessment will be ongoing.

require diagnosis and medical management as well. In such a case, a psychiatrist must also be part of the team to assess whether seizures might contribute to the regression seen in some students with autism.

Review of Assessments

Once all the assessments have been completed and the reports distributed, the entire school team, including the parents, should meet to review the results and determine if any further assessment is necessary. It is important to provide a coherent picture of the student's strengths and difficulties, and this is best achieved through combining the findings of the interdisciplinary team into one report (Klin, Carter, Volkmar, Cohen, Marans, & Sparrow, 1997). Because of the complex nature of ASD, it is crucial to allow plenty of time for parents' questions and to promote discussion of their student's needs and strengths. It will be helpful if everyone assumes the position of wanting to understand the student as best as possible, so if you find you have questions about something that was said or of the test results, be sure to ask—the parents probably have the same questions.

Below is a summary of John's evaluation results that were shared with his parents and with all his teachers. The evaluation was conducted by school staff over a six-week period and included a summary of his developmental history and information from his pediatric psychiatrist.

Evaluation Summary

Name: John Lee   Age: 8.10   Grade: 3rd

This is a summary of the assessment results compiled by John Lee's special education team from the individual reports provided for each of the areas evaluated.

Medical and Developmental History

John was a healthy baby and appeared to meet all physical developmental milestones. However, as a toddler, parents noted the following concerns:

- Frequent tantrums especially when something unexpected or out of the routine occurred
- Slow to talk
- Barely toilet trained by his fifth birthday
- Picky eater

In first grade, he was diagnosed with ADHD and prescribed Adderall to help him focus in school. Parents' current concerns include the following:

- Sensitivity to noise and touch
- Easily frustrated
- Trouble independently completing simple tasks, such as getting dressed in the morning
- Prefers the company of either adults or much younger children
- Appears much younger emotionally
- Often prefers to simply go to his room to be by himself

Psychological and Behavioral

The school psychologist reported the following:

- *The Wechsler Intelligence Scale for Children, Fourth Edition* (WISC-IV) (Wechsler, 2003): verbal comprehension index 88, perceptual reasoning index 112, working memory index 113, processing speed index 87, and full scale IQ 100. The significantly different performance IQ scores indicate that John has average to above-average cognitive ability.
- *The Gilliam Autism Rating Scale, Second Edition* (GARS-2) (Gilliam, 2006): The results showed significant findings for autism in stereotyped behaviors, communication, and social interaction. The total autism index of 125 indicated a high probability of autism.
- *The Behavior Assessment System for Children, Second Edition* (BASC-2) (Reynolds & Kamphaus, 1992): The results show a marked improvement of behavior when medicated but persistent difficulties with emotional self-control deficits, lack of resiliency, withdrawal, ineffective executive functioning system, weak ego strength, hyperactivity, social skills and functional communication deficits, and problems with adaptability and daily living skills.

Academics

The special education teacher gathered information from the classroom teacher, from district-wide assessments, and also administered the WJ III. The results from the WJ III confirm that John has delayed reading fluency and comprehension skills; he is below his peers in basic writing skills and in math calculation skills. The WJ III was administered over several days to allow for frequent breaks when he had difficulty attending or when he became frustrated by the task.

Communication and Social

The SLP collected a language sample which revealed age-appropriate phonological development but delays in both his ability to answer questions and sustain a conversation. Additionally, his speech has a high pitch, a monotone quality, and a loudness level that often does not match the social situation. He has flat affect, seldom makes eye contact, and has few interactions with peers.

- *The Clinical Evaluation of Language Fundamentals, Fourth Edition* (CELF-4) (Semel, Wiig, & Secord, 2003) revealed significant delays in expressive language but near average receptive language ability; his strengths are in vocabulary knowledge and understanding the structure of the language; he has difficulty with answering questions, making inferences, and the abstract use of language.
- *The Test of Pragmatic Language, Second Edition* (TOPL-2) (Phelps-Terasaki & Phelps-Gunn, 2007) showed deficits in each of the six core subcomponents of pragmatic language evaluated: physical setting, audience, topic, purpose (speech acts), visual-gestural cues, and abstraction.

His teachers and peers report that John gets irritated quickly if anyone comes very close to him and complains that people are being mean to him. On the playground, he usually plays by himself. Change of any sort is difficult for him; he does best when routines and structures are maintained.

(Continued)

(Continued)

Motor Skills and Physical Assessment

John is left-handed and handwriting skills are good. The main concern in the area of gross motor skills is his lack of coordination with catching and throwing a ball and a somewhat odd running gait. Assessments by both the PT and OT showed low muscle tone but adequate functional motor skills. He passed both his vision and hearing tests.

Sensory

The OT collected the following information:

- The sensory profile caretaker questionnaire pinpointed three areas of definite sensory developmental differences: auditory filtering, tactile sensitivity, and taste/smell sensitivity. Noise interferes with his ability to complete tasks and pay attention, which causes him to miss out on important information. John can only wear certain clothes; reacts as if in pain when hair is washed, combed, or cut; has trouble standing in line close to others; reacts strongly when touched but enjoys touching other people and often in ways that surprise them, such as stroking their hair. John's sensitivity to smells makes it hard for him to enter the lunch room and eat with his peers, and he will only eat certain foods.

Conclusions

The data gathered by school professionals through observation, testing, and parent report reveals significant social and behavioral difficulties, communication differences, and sensory issues. The convergence of this data supports a diagnosis of autism and qualifies him to receive special education services.

Recommendations

The school team's recommendations are as follows:

- An IEP to provide direct special education services in the areas of expressive and pragmatic language, sensory integration, reading, writing, math, and social skills
- Positive behavioral supports should be in place and his environment monitored to reduce his exposure to noise, crowding, and smells (e.g., he may need to eat away from the lunchroom)
- A Circle of Friends—a small group of typical peers, John and an adult facilitator meeting on a weekly basis to engage in some fun activity through which both John and peers can come to better understand each other
- One-on-one social skill training
- A home base he can go to when he is feeling overwhelmed in the classroom—a place where he can get emotional support and assistance with his academic work
- Paraprofessional support to help him stay on task in the general education setting
- Visual supports and hands-on activities should be used as much as possible
- A visual schedule should be used to help reduce anxiety, and a change in routine should be reflected in this schedule
- Reinforcement strategies should be used to increase his motivation to engage in academic and social tasks

3

Getting Ready to Teach New Skills

Basic First Steps

Danielle, a five-year-old with autism, is nonverbal, and not yet toilet trained. Her educational team completed a thorough evaluation and determined that overall Danielle's skills lag far behind those of her peers. They concluded that Danielle needs to acquire new skills in the areas of socialization, academics, behavior, communication, and self-help skills. However, because she seems to have an endless list of needs, the team is almost at a loss on where to begin, how to prioritize her needs, how many objectives to target for teaching, and so forth. They feel almost paralyzed by the scope of the problem.

In the previous chapter, we discussed the evaluation and assessment process required to provide a comprehensive picture of a student's academic, social, and overall developmental standing. Armed with this information, you are now ready to design an educational program for your student. Regardless of the difficulties your student faces, whether there are just a few or many new skills to teach, it is always vitally important to engage in the intervention process in a systematic and thoughtful fashion. To aid you in this process, this chapter discusses

- how to choose objectives for your student,
- how to write individualized educational plan (IEP) goals,
- how to find curriculum resources,

- how to use staff resources to implement the interventions, and
- how to compile a binder to organize your entire program of intervention.

Choosing Objectives

Once you are familiar with your student's strengths and needs, you are ready to choose the specific skills you will be targeting for the IEP. As you design this program, you will want to capitalize on the student's strengths and use them to teach new skills. Because there is frequently a huge gap between the developmental level of a student with autism spectrum disorder (ASD) and that of the typical peer, you may find it difficult to prioritize which objectives to choose first. One way to simplify the process is to look at areas of development and choose goals for each one. Typically, all students need assistance in academics, behavior (including life skills), and communication, which you would consider as the crucial core components of an educational plan. Here are some guidelines as you consider the specific objectives for each area:

- Be realistic in the number of goals you write. If you try to tackle too many goals, you will become overwhelmed.
- At the same time, do not underestimate the amount of progress a student can make when best practices are in place.
- Be realistic in the type of goals you select. Choose ones that your student has the greatest chances of acquiring; success is always motivating for both teacher and student.
- Choose goals for which your student has the prerequisite skills. The goal of using complete sentences to answer questions, for example, will be chosen after a student has acquired the ability to put three or four words together.
- Choose goals that give your student access to reinforcers. If, for example, turning on a radio will allow a student access to the music that he loves, then independently operating a radio might be a worthwhile skill to teach.
- Choose goals that are developmentally and chronologically appropriate for your student.
- Choose goals that focus on the student's interests and take advantage of his or her strengths. If, for example, a preschool student is fascinated by letters, teach him to read; if an elementary student is eager to be first at everything, use this desire to teach the student how to *appropriately* tell peers when it is time to move to a new activity.
- Choose goals that are prerequisites for other important skills. For example, teaching keyboarding skills will allow a student to complete assignments on an AlphaSmart or on a computer.
- Choose goals that have the potential to reduce or eliminate problem behaviors. Teaching a student how to use a calculator, for example, may eliminate shouting out in frustration when doing certain problems in math class.

- Choose goals that promote independence. Teaching a student to follow a visual activity schedule, for example, will allow him to independently participate in home activities such as baking, emptying the dishwasher, cleaning his or her room, and so forth.

Writing an IEP Goal

Once the goals are chosen, be specific when you describe them in the student's IEP, making sure to use observable and measurable terms. You will also want to delineate exactly what you consider as mastery of a goal. Here are several examples of IEP goals:

Goal: By 1/30/2009, Kate will independently complete 2nd-grade morning worksheets within 10 minutes with no more than two verbal prompts 95% of the time as measured by data on 10 consecutive days.

Goal: By 1/30/2009, Kate will walk quietly in the school hallways 90% of the time as measured by data on five consecutive days.

Goal: By 1/30/2009, Kate will answer "what," "where," "when," and "who" questions, after reading one paragraph section of the 2nd-grade language arts book, 80% correctly as measured by responses to questions over two different paragraphs on five consecutive days.

Goal: By 1/30/2009, Kate will initiate verbal interactions with peers or respond verbally to their interactions at least five times each recess, 80% of the time, as measured during each of the three daily recess times on three consecutive data collection days.

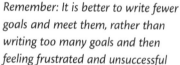

Remember: It is better to write fewer goals and meet them, rather than writing too many goals and then feeling frustrated and unsuccessful because the objectives are too ambitious for the student to master.

Curriculum Resources

Several curriculum resources have been developed to specifically address the unique needs of students with ASD. We hope that Table 3.1 will help you decide which curriculum is the best fit for your student's needs.

Implementing the Interventions

Once the student's goals have been determined and the basic approach to intervention agreed upon, the next step is to delineate who will implement the program. The multidisciplinary team must discuss how to meet the student's needs and how to make progress through an intense and well-coordinated

Table 3.1 Curriculum Resources

Resource	Social/ Communication	Academics	Self-Help	Language	Behavior	Developmental Level
DO-WATCH-LISTEN-SAY: Social and Communication Intervention for Children With Autism (Quill, 2000)	√			√		Beginning
Relationship Development Intervention With Young Children (Gutstein & Sheely, 2002b)	√					Beginning
Relationship Development Intervention With Children, Adolescents, and Adults (Gutstein & Sheely, 2002a)	√					Intermediate and Advanced
Teach Me Language (Freeman & Dake, 1997a)	√	√		√		Intermediate and Advanced
Thinking About You Thinking About Me (Winner, 2002)	√					Intermediate and Advanced
Behavioral Intervention for Young Children With Autism: A Manual for Parents and Professionals (Maurice, Green, & Luce, 1996)	√	√	√	√	√	Beginning, Intermediate, and Advanced
A Work in Progress: Behavior Management Strategies and a Curriculum for Intensive Behavioral Treatment of Autism (Leaf & McEachin, 1999)	√	√	√	√	√	Beginning and Intermediate

Resource	Social/Communication	Academics	Self-Help	Language	Behavior	Developmental Level
The Affect-Based Language Curriculum (ABLC) (Greenspan & Lewis, 2005).	√			√	√	Beginning
Making a Difference: Behavioral Intervention for Autism (Maurice, Green, & Foxx, 2001)	√				√	Beginning and Intermediate
Asperger's . . . What Does It Mean to Me? (Faherty, 2000)	√					Intermediate and Advanced
Room 14: A Social Language Program (Wilson, 1993)	√					Intermediate (ages 6–10)
Room 28: A Social Language Program (LoGiudice & McConnell, 2004)	√					Advanced (ages 12–18)
Autism and PDD Social Skills Lessons Series (Reese & Challenner, 1999)			√			Beginning, Intermediate, and Advanced
Navigating the Social World (McAfee, 2002)						Intermediate and Advanced
The Language of Perspective Taking (Toomey, 2002)	√					Intermediate and Advanced
Teaching Children With Autism to Mind-Read (Howlin, Baron-Cohen, & Hadwin, 1999)	√					Intermediate and Advanced

effort. Many goals should be worked on throughout the day rather than at one fixed time, thus requiring a number of different staff, and even parents, to work together on different objectives.

Paraeducators may provide the continual support that will be needed to teach the student to follow a schedule, to request breaks when appropriate, to learn the basics of classroom rules and behavior, to listen to the classroom teacher, to initiate with peers, and to respond appropriately to others. In some instances, it will be necessary to train paraeducators to also teach students one-on-one. Team teaching—where special education staff and the regular education teacher join forces—may be necessary to provide a consistent and intense learning environment for the student. As is often the case, approaches that assist students with ASD are also beneficial for all students.

The Binder

Now that you have identified the specific skills that need to be addressed for your student, it is time to get organized. The first thing that you will need to get started is a 2.5- or a 3-inch binder. Put the student's name and the current school year on the side and on the front of the binder. At least eight dividers will initially be needed with the following labels:

- Student's IEP and, when necessary, a medical plan, list of dietary restrictions, and a behavior plan
- Daily schedule (includes who works with the student, at what time, the location and activity, and the sensory break times and activities)
- Classroom: behavioral, life skills, social, and communication objectives data form
- Direct instruction programs
- Home-school communication forms
- Regular team meeting minutes
- Extra blank forms

A checklist of the sections needed in a binder is provided in Resource B.

Student's IEP

Because a student's IEP is an important legal document that dictates his or her educational programs, it should be shared with all who work with the student, especially the paraeducators. Other school staff, such as bus drivers, monitors, secretaries, and lunchroom staff, who come in contact with the student, should be made aware of the student's difficulties and how to provide the best support.

Remember: Just like all other academic skills, adaptive behaviors require systematic and explicit teaching.

Daily Schedule

The daily schedule is especially important information when a student works with a number of teachers and has many goals to accomplish. This schedule should be attached to the inside cover of the binder, and it includes the following information:

- The person working with the student
- The time and place of the activity
- The type of activity (e.g., academic, communication, social, or sensory)
- The targeted goal

See a sample of a daily schedule in Figure 3.1. You can also format a table on your own computer that works for your student's needs and can be easily updated. A blank form of various formats for a daily schedule is provided in Resource C.

Classroom Objectives

Oftentimes, in addition to the academic IEP objectives, teachers have other objectives for their students related to everyday classroom adaptive behaviors, such as the ability to independently get off a bus, walk to the classroom, hang up a coat, join in the other peers' activities, and so forth. To ensure that a student makes progress on all of these fronts, it is essential to measure his or her skill in each area. Measuring a student's performance throughout the day ensures that the attention is focused on teaching the required skills and doing it in the natural context when possible. See Figure 3.2 for a sample of a data collection form that might help you keep track of these skills. You will find in Resource D a blank form that you can duplicate for your own use.

The example above refers to a young student but the same approach can be used for students at any developmental level, including those in high school. For a secondary aged student, you might have objectives divided into classroom behavior (e.g., raises hand to answer questions, keeps head off desk, and follows teacher's directions), hallway behavior (e.g., walks, keeps hands and feet to self, and responds to students greetings and questions), lunchroom behavior (e.g., keeps food on tray, sits with at least one peer, and asks to leave when necessary) and homework completion (e.g., writes in planner, checks backpack before going home for homework assignments, and gives homework to special education teacher before first hour). You can use the blank form in Resource D to monitor progress on these objectives.

Programs

This is the place where you will want to keep a record of the curricula and the specific skills you plan to teach throughout the year. It is helpful to separate the programs with dividers and to include in each the following information:

- Student's specific curricula
- Data collection forms

Figure 3.1   A Sample of a Preschool Student's Daily Schedule

Daily Schedule

Student's Name: Rosie Brown   **Date:** Oct. 2008

Time	Place	Person				Activities/Goals
		Mon	*Tues*	*Wed*	*Thur*	
8:30	Classroom	Lisa	Sarah	Lisa	Sarah	Hang up backpack, greet peers, adults
8:45	DI room	Lisa	Sarah	Lisa	Sarah	Speech/Language programs, priming for day
9:05	Hallway	Lisa	Sarah	Lisa	Sarah	Sensory break—jumping on the trampoline
9:10	Classroom	Lisa	Sarah	Lisa	Sarah	Center time—use schedule, participate alongside peers, fine motor goals, and turn-taking
9:40	Teacher's office	Teacher	Teacher	Teacher	Teacher	Sensory break—quiet time on bean bag listening to music, priming for circle time
9:50	Classroom	Lisa	Sarah	Lisa	Sarah	Circle time—sit independently and choose a song (using picture exchange communication system [PECS])
10:00	DI room	Lisa	Sarah	Lisa	Sarah	Speech/language programs
10:25	DI room	Lisa	Sarah	Lisa	Sarah	Sensory break—carry books to library and back
10:35	Classroom	Lisa	Sarah	Lisa	Sarah	Snack—sit independently and request food (using PECS)
10:50	Outside	Lisa	Sarah	Lisa	Sarah	Play—use schedule to direct activities, take turns, follow one step directions
11:20	DI room	Renae	Renae	Renae	Renae	Preacademic skills
11:50	Classroom	Lisa	Sarah	Lisa	Sarah	Prepare to go home, say goodbye to peers

Figure 3.2   Classroom Objectives

Student's Name: _____   Date: _____

	Monday	Tuesday	Wednesday	Thursday	Friday
Arrival					
Hang up coat	+	+	−	+	+
Hang up bag	−	−	−	−	−
Say "hi" to one adult	−	−	−	+	+
Say "hi" to one peer	−	−	−	+	−
Washing Hands					
Wet hands	−	−	−	−	−
Rub soap on hands	+	+	+	+	+
Rinse hands	+	+	+	+	+
Dry hands	+	−	+	+	+
Meal Time					
Take plate and utensils to the table	+	−	−	+	+
Answer with "yes/no" and "thank you" when asked "Do you want _____?"	−	−	+	+	+
Request food (using picture exchange communication system [PECS])	−	−	−	+	+
Clean up	−	−	−	−	−
Circle Time					
Sit independently	+	+	+	+	+
Choose song (using PECS)	−	+	+	−	−
Imitate actions 50% of the time	+	+	+	+	+

- Graphs
- Plastic pockets, when needed, to hold relevant materials (e.g., cards)

For example, a student's programs might consist of receptive and expressive language, math, social, and self-help skills. The expressive language program might require a student to acquire competency in such skills as answering yes/no questions. This program will, therefore, consist of a list of suggested strategies along with data collection forms to monitor a student's progress in this domain. Several examples of forms that might help you keep track of the skills needed to be taught and to monitor progress are offered in Resource E.

Home-School Communication

Consistent communication between home and school is vital especially when you have a student who is young or low functioning. Steady communication between teacher and parents can alleviate the natural anxieties parents might have as well as having a positive impact on a student's functioning at school and on his or her transition to home. Ultimately, good communication between parents and teacher contributes to a relationship of trust and increases the student's performance at school.

The communication between parents and teachers can take several forms. Many teachers and parents prefer using a notebook that goes back and forth between school and home. Another possibility could be a simple form, such as the ones illustrated in Resource F. As you can see from the examples provided in this resource, some forms may be designed for the use of parents and teacher, exclusively. Others may be designed to include a student's input and encourage his or her involvement. The design and level of detail in such a form depend on the age of the student and his or her developmental level. Typically, at the end of the school day, the teacher and the student fill out this form together. When the form is used to both inform the parents and provide a basis for communication with their child, the student may practice his or her answers before leaving for home. At home, the student's parents ask the questions, using the form, to help their child remember the day's activities.

Remember: The answers written in those forms are at the language level the student is capable of using independently.

Regular Team Meeting Minutes

Regular monthly, bimonthly, or weekly team meetings are often needed to keep everyone informed of the student's progress and brainstorm solutions for possible challenges that might arise. Because teachers' time is very limited, and the student's challenges may be numerous, it is advisable to strive for maximum efficiency at these meetings. Here are some ideas to consider:

1. Collect agenda items. Those items should be very specific and limited in number. If at all possible, team members should be notified of the items to allow them to think and come prepared with ideas.

2. The meetings should have a specific beginning and ending time. Typically, when participants are aware of the time restraints, they match their comments accordingly, and as a result, the discussion becomes focused.

3. When you consider whom to invite to these meetings, remember that paraeducators are an essential part of a student's team and are major contributors to the success of any intervention. And, of course, it is also strongly recommended that you include parents in these meetings as much as possible. Parents' involvement in any treatment is key to its success.

4. Record the decisions made to ensure that they will be implemented. In addition, if similar challenges are faced at a later time, these notes will help team members find out how they were handled in the past. It is advisable, therefore, to devise a way of recording who is going to do what (e.g., who will order the new writing materials). See a sample of such a recording system in Resource G, and your school may have its own form of recording the minutes.

Remember: Each team member should receive a copy of the decisions, as a reminder of the tasks assigned to every participant.

Blank Forms

It might be frustrating for a teacher to have a student sitting nicely in a chair and ready to start work, only to realize that there are not enough data collection forms for use during the new lesson. It is thus recommended to have a special section in the binder for extra copies of all data forms that are being typically used.

Of course, other information pertinent to a successful school day, such as the results of a reinforcement survey, should be included in the binder. The binder is, if you like, a working document that contains not only the goals and objectives of the student's educational plan, but also stores the daily data, weekly graphs, and the results of discussions and communication with home—these all serve to organize and drive an effective program.

This concludes our discussion of the organizational aspect of our teaching. It is time now to look back at Danielle from our vignette. Based on the discussion above, how would you prioritize the teaching of objectives for Danielle? Which skills would you target first? Danielle's parents and her teachers are keenly aware of the narrow window of opportunity for teaching her new skills, especially in the communication area. Because Danielle is nonverbal, the team decided to focus on teaching her to communicate using the picture exchange communication system (PECS). To help her integrate into her general education classroom, the team also decided to target toilet training.

Now that you have the organizational tools in place, we can direct our attention toward environmental issues that are key ingredients to the successful implementation of any program.

4

Environmental Supports

Mike is a 12-year-old with an autism spectrum disorder (ASD). He participates during most of the day in his general education class. However, lately Mike has been in trouble several times because he skipped assemblies and failed to tell his teacher where he was going; Mike just disappeared. When asked by his teacher why he did not come to the assembly, he did not answer. This behavior has persisted despite being repeatedly reprimanded.

❖

Our experience from working with students with ASD has taught us that learning and behavior can be greatly enhanced by environmental supports, such as visual aids, the structuring of space and time, and sensory interventions. This chapter discusses these issues in detail and offers specific strategies in each area that can be used in any classroom. Remember, it is most helpful if each member of the student's educational team joins forces to ensure that all environmental supports are in place.

Visual Aids

As you think of the difficulties people with autism have functioning in their environment, it may be helpful for you to imagine that one day you found yourself in a totally different culture. You would find the language, the social expectations, and the daily routine to be completely foreign to you. You might even be disoriented by the different sounds and smells. Would you know what to say, what to do, where to go, and what came next? How would you find food to eat? How would you find a bathroom? What is in the environment that could make life easier for you? Would visuals help you find your way around? Would you feel more or less secure if things looked orderly?

Certainly, for example, pictures of food items on the menu would help you order a meal you might enjoy. A series of pictures depicting the different activities of the day would ease your anxiety, as it would show you what to expect. In a public place, you would be glad to see a picture of a man or a woman on a door that would let you know which restroom to use. You get the picture!

Temple Grandin, the world-famous high-functioning adult with autism, states, "I think in pictures. Words are like a second language to me" (Grandin, 1996, p. 19). It is, therefore, crucial to have a well-thought-out system of visual supports in place to assist the student in the autism spectrum. The visual supports described below include visual transition schedules, visual work schedules, visual cues, and labeling.

Visual Transition Schedules

Visual transition schedules are an absolute must for all students in the autism spectrum. In fact, this support is important to everyone. You and I check our planners for appointments, and if we go to an all-day event we expect to be given an agenda that at least tells us the location, the topics, the names of the speakers, and when there is a break for coffee or lunch. In schools, teachers typically have a schedule on the blackboard so that all their students know what to expect during the day. However, students in the autism spectrum need to have their very own schedule that they can

Remember: All students with autism should have a schedule of their own, regardless of how well they function in their environment.

refer to frequently during the day. Indeed, it is strongly recommended that each student have a visual schedule in place the very first day of class. Transition schedules have the following purposes: to assist students' transition from one activity to another independently; to alleviate anxiety by showing the major transitions of the day; to communicate changes in the routines; to translate in concrete language abstract concepts, such as art; and finally, to increase students' sense of control over their daily activities.

The design of a transition schedule requires some thought, so before making one, here are some issues to keep in mind:

- *Portability*—Is your student moving from one classroom to another frequently during the day? If so, consider a schedule that can be easily carried by the student from one location to another.
- *Age Appropriateness*—Schedules should look socially acceptable. After all, in inclusive settings we want the students with ASD to blend in with their peers.
- *Developmental Appropriateness*—It is important to ensure that the student can use a schedule with minimal teaching. Thus, for example, for a non-reader, the schedule would rely primarily on pictures.

- *Functionality*—All schedules should be manipulated by the students themselves. Thus, we need to consider questions, such as whether students can manipulate them with their fingers or with their hand, can hold on to them to transport to the new location (if they are using crutches, for example), can easily access a pen to write on them if that is required, and so forth. Other issues that can make a schedule user friendly are the size of the icons and the direction of the items on the schedule: Should they go in a horizontal or in a vertical direction?

There are three different kinds of schedules for you to consider: (1) an object schedule, (2) a picture schedule, or (3) a written schedule. The choice of schedule for a specific student will be based on what is clearest for him or her.

OBJECT SCHEDULES

If your student does not yet understand how a picture can stand for an object, you will need to provide him with an object schedule.

How to Make an Object Schedule

Use miniature-sized objects or life-sized objects placed in compartments, such as a shoe organizer, or Velcroed on to a laminated paper grid that goes from left to right. For example, a toothbrush can symbolize brushing teeth, a cup can represent snack time, and a ball can signal outside time, and so on. Make sure to always have the name of the activity the object represents written under each object (see Figure 4.1).

Figure 4.1   Object Transition Schedule

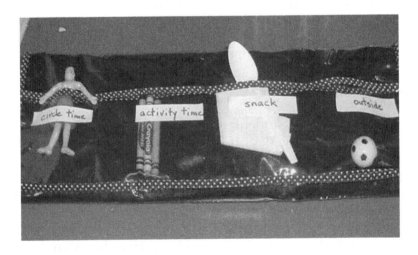

How to Use an Object Transition Schedule

First, tell your student, "Check the schedule," or ask, "What's next?" Then physically assist the student from behind to pick up the item and transport it to the correct location until the student can do so independently. If the student is not going to use the specific item once he or she gets there, make sure to design a place for him to place it.

PICTURE SCHEDULES

If your student understands that a picture or an icon can represent an activity but is not yet a fluent reader, the student's schedule should be made using pictures or icons with the written word included. Whether to use photographs, a picture, or an icon that represents the activity depends on the student's developmental level. One of the most popular softwares used in schools to create a picture schedule is Boardmaker. Pictures and icons can also be downloaded for free at these websites: http://www.classroomclipart.com/ and http://office.microsoft.com/en-us/clipart/default.aspx. Many students do well with the simplicity of an icon, which does not have the background distracters present in photographs. Black and white icons may work just as well as colored ones. There are basically two types of picture schedules: fixed schedules and portable schedules.

Fixed Schedules

Fixed schedules are useful when a student spends most of his time in one location. These schedules can be either taped to the student's desk or mounted on a wall or a door, and they can contain either moveable icons or icons that are printed in a list format. The section below describes two variations for the use of a fixed schedule.

FIXED SCHEDULES WITH MOVEABLE ICONS

How to Make a Fixed Schedule With Moveable Icons

Laminate a strip of cardboard; attach a strip of Velcro in the middle. Mount the icons of the activities at the top of white index cards when used with library pockets (as described below). Otherwise, mount the pictures on construction paper. All icons should be laminated for durability. Put a piece of Velcro (the opposite kind of what you used on the long strip) on their back side. Place the pictures on the strip of Velcro in the order that the activities will occur either from left to right or vertically.

Figure 4.2   A Fixed Schedule With
Moveable Icons

Make a container to house the pictures the student removes when he or she checks his or her schedule. There are two types of containers: all pictures container or the destination container. The all pictures container (see Figure 4.2) is placed beside the schedule strip, and here are examples of containers that work well: small coffee can with a slit in the plastic lid, a laminated manila envelope, or a milk carton with the top cut off. If used to contain pictures after completing an activity, write ALL DONE or FINISHED on the container.

A destination container (see Figure 4.3) is placed at each location of an activity to house only the relevant picture. (This system is recommended for students who are novice schedule users and who need help to focus on their next activity or destination.) The destination container consists of a laminated library pocket with a matching picture on the front that is Velcroed or taped in a visible place at the location of the activity.

How to Use a Fixed Schedule With Moveable Icons and a Destination Container

There are three basic ways to use a fixed schedule with moveable icons: (1) The student removes the icon from the schedule strip and carries it to the location of the next activity and places it in the pocket or on the Velcro spot; (2) the student removes the icon from the schedule, immediately places it in the all pictures container, and then proceeds to that activity; or (3) upon completing an activity, the student returns to the schedule, removes the icon representing the last activity, places it in the all pictures container labeled finished, and then checks the schedule for the next activity.

If the student still needs to carry the picture as a reminder where to go as he or she transitions but does not need help to find the right location, you can place a Velcro strip at that spot for the child to place the picture on. When he is finished with the activity, he takes the picture back to the schedule, drops it in a finished container, and checks the schedule for the next activity.

Figure 4.3   A Fixed Schedule With Moveable Icons and a Destination Container

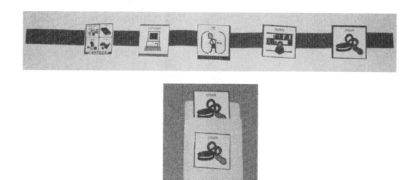

FIXED PICTURE SCHEDULES IN A LIST FORMAT

A transition schedule that is one step prior to the written schedule is one in which the icons along with the corresponding word are in a list format, and there is a box by each item.

How to Make a Fixed Picture Schedule in a List Format

Print out the icons representing the activities in a list format. Laminate or place the list in a sheet protector, tape the schedule on the student's desk. Velcro a dry erase pen to the schedule to ensure the student can always find it.

How to Use a Fixed Picture Schedule in a List Format

Teach the student to put a checkmark through the picture or in a box beside the picture once the activity is completed.

Portable Schedules

Portable schedules are useful for students who move frequently throughout the day between classes. There are two types of portable schedules: the moveable icons schedule and the written schedule in a list format.

Figure 4.4   The Manila Folder Schedule

The Moveable Icon Schedule

There are two popular portable schedules using moveable icons: the manila folder and the album.

THE MANILA FOLDER

How to Make a Portable Schedule With a Manila Folder

Laminate the folder. Place a Velcro strip along one length of the folder with the word schedule above it. Print icons along with words to represent activities or location. Mount the icons on construction paper, laminate, and put a piece of Velcro on the back of each. Place the icons on the Velcro strip from left to right in the order of the activities. On the other side of the folder, attach a laminated envelope with the word finished on it. Another method is to place a strip of Velcro with the word finished above it on the other side of the manila folder (see Figure 4.4).

How to Use a Portable Manila Folder Schedule

When an activity is completed, the student takes the picture off the schedule and puts it in the finished envelope or places it on the finished Velcro strip.

THE PHOTO ALBUM

The album can be used when students are distracted by seeing all the activities listed for the day at one time.

How to Make a Portable Schedule With an Album

Using a small photo album, roughly six inches by six inches, a size easily carried by the student, place tag board or other stiff paper inside each plastic pocket. Make the icons as described above. Place Velcro on each plastic pocket and strips of Velcro on the back cover and the last plastic pocket.

How to Use a Portable Album Schedule

When an activity is completed, the student takes the picture off the page and places it on the back page.

THE WRITTEN SCHEDULE

Written schedules are used with students who are confident in their reading ability.

How to Make a Written Schedule

This schedule can simply be a list of the activities (e.g., recess, math, reading, lunch), or it can include the time, place, room number, teacher (e.g., 9:00 a.m.– Math–Room 102–Mrs. Smith), along with a box (see Figure 4.5). This page can be either laminated or placed in a sheet protector. A dry erase marker should be attached to the schedule to ensure availability when the student needs it.

Figure 4.5   The Written Schedule

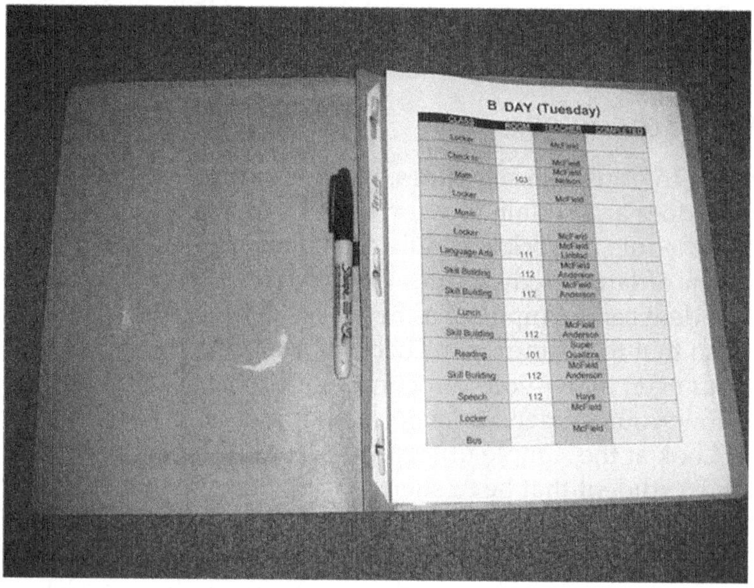

How to Use a Written Schedule

Teach the student to cross off the activity after he or she has completed it and is about to transition to the next one. Here are general guidelines for using a schedule:

- The size of the icons depends on the student's age and developmental level.
- In the beginning, to avoid overwhelming the student, put only a few of the pictures on the schedule.
- Before issuing the instruction "Check your schedule" or "What's next," make sure you have the student's attention.
- Refrain from repeating the instruction. Rather, allow the student enough time to process the instruction.
- Use physical assistance when teaching students to follow a schedule. Research shows that, unlike verbal prompts, the physical ones are easier to fade.
- Fade the physical prompts gradually to ensure the student's success (see Chapter 5 for a discussion on prompt fading).
- Plan to fade the physical prompts as soon as possible.

Remember: Students with ASD may take a long time to process and respond to auditory information— sometimes up to 45 seconds!

At the end of the day, it is the teacher's responsibility to ensure that the schedule is ready for use the next day. In other words, it is the teacher's responsibility to collect the icons from the various locations or to clean a schedule that has been marked on.

Visual Work Schedules

In contrast to transition schedules, work schedules list the different activities a student does at a certain location or steps in a given activity. Similarly to a transition schedule, a work schedule can be either pictorial or written. It can be in the form of laminated pictures or words, attached by Velcro to a strip, which the student can manipulate as he or she completes each step, or it can be printed out so that the student can checkmark each completed segment. Work schedules can even allow you to incorporate choice. You might, for instance, use it to allow your student to choose the order of the activities he or she engages in. Look at the sample in Figure 4.6. In this illustration, there are three icons that tell a student that he or she needs to work on matching, sorting, and bead patterns. The space underneath is divided in two sections: start and finished. On the left-hand side, the student places the icons in the order that the student chooses to perform those activities. As he or she completes each task, he or she transfers its icon to the right-hand side, labeled finished.

Sometimes, it may be possible for you to even allow the student to choose which activities to do on a given day. Consider the following example: Assume that your student needs to work on the following five areas: verbs, addition, coloring, cutting, and vocabulary. Laminate and Velcro each one of these words and place them on a strip of Velcro on cardboard. Underneath it

Figure 4.6   Visual Work Schedule

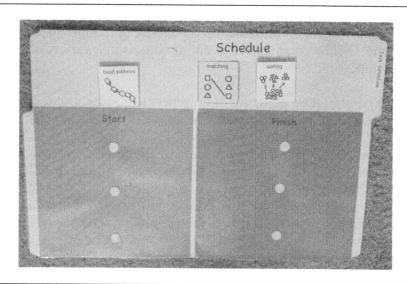

you may write, "Today I work on," and below that draw four squares. Place a piece of Velcro in each square. Ask the student to choose, from the five activities above, which four that he or she would like to work on. If the student always avoids the same activity, you can overcome this problem by placing that activity in one of the four squares. Then the student still has an opportunity to choose the other three activities.

Often there is no choice available to the student because he or she is part of a larger group. In this case, it is still important to provide the group's schedule to your student. Teachers typically write the schedule on the board, so be sure that your student with ASD can see it, and if you verbally change the schedule, be sure that it is put in writing for him or her.

Visual Cues

Visual cues translate everyday information, usually picked up readily by most students, into a language understood by students in the autism spectrum. Visual cues can clarify the environment to our students; they can show expectations and whether or not their performance is acceptable or correct. Visual cues are designed to foster a student's independence, to increase understanding or control over the environment, and to prompt initiations for requesting help. Visual cues can include body stance, hand signs, facial expression, color coding, placement of objects in the environment, as well as written and pictorial cues. The decision to use visual cues and the decision as to which ones to use will depend on the situations that are troublesome to the student. Here are some examples:

THE UNIVERSAL PICTORIAL "NO" SYMBOL

We have found this symbol to be very effective in communicating to our students what is allowed and what is out of bounds in a variety of situations, such as the following:

- It can be placed on a picture of an action (e.g., kicking) and held up to tell the student to stop whatever he or she is doing, rather than repeatedly telling the student to stop.
- It can be placed over a schedule item to let the student know that there is a change and this activity will not be part of his or her day.
- It can be placed over a picture in the student's picture exchange communication system (PECS) book to tell him or her that this choice is not available at this time, rather than removing the picture.
- It can be placed on a door to tell the student that he or she may not use that exit, or it can be placed on the entrance to an activity area to say that it is out of bounds.

COLOR CODING

Color coding is a simple visual strategy that helps organize a student's environment.

- It can mark a student's personal area. Everything that denotes the student's belongings or area for work can be labeled and can have the same background color paper (name on circle time mat, work area, cubby, chair, basket for papers, etc.).
- It can help students organize their papers by subject matter in different file folders and in-out baskets.
- Highlighters of various colors can be used by teachers to mark for students which papers are homework and which are class notes to study from.

MASKING TAPE

- A strip of masking tape across the floor inside the door reminds students to stay inside the room until given permission to leave.
- An outline of a square or circle with masking tape can be used to show a student where to sit or where to play.
- Color-coded masking tape can provide an additional cue to mark a student's seat and the location of his or her materials.

GESTURES, BODY POSITIONING, AND FACIAL EXPRESSIONS

Hand gestures, body positioning, and facial expressions are natural cues that all of us use throughout the day to convey meaning to our words. Many students with ASD who cannot solely rely on auditory information can benefit from the use of these tools when used consciously and explicitly in situations such as the ones described below:

- A teacher's raised hand can be used to mean "Look at me!"
- The wave of the arm can signal "Come here."
- Pointing to the materials can focus the student's attention.
- The exaggerated use of facial expressions along with thumbs up can be used to indicate approval of student.
- Simply pausing, or blocking a student from continuing in his or her activity, or opening one's eyes wide signals to the student that something is required of him or her in this situation.
- To signal a student that he or she should raise or lower the volume of his or her voice, you can raise or lower your open hand.

ROOM LIGHT

You can turn lights off or on in class to gain students' attention and to signal transitions. Turning the light off may be used as a calming technique or to help students focus in on certain tasks.

CUE CARDS

Use cue cards to prompt speech, rather than repeatedly telling the student, "Matt, say . . . ." Cue cards are effective for teaching greetings such as "hi" and "bye," pronouns "I" and "you," and expressions such as "my turn" and "your turn" during games.

SENTENCE STRIPS

Sentence strips can be used to prompt social initiations, such as "What is your name?" and "What are you doing?" When a student's conversational skills become more fluent, sentence strips can be faded by gradually omitting parts of the sentence until they consist of only circles or squares that stand for each word, which can also be eventually completely removed.

WRITTEN RULES, 5-POINT SCALE, POWER CARDS, AND SOCIAL STORIES

Written rules, the 5-Point Scale, Power Cards, and Social Stories work well for good readers and can be placed on the student's desk or inside his or her planner. Examples of such rules are "Keep my hands to myself," "Look at the person I am talking to," "Don't say more than five things about my favorite subject." The 5-Point Scale, Power Cards, and Social Stories are all discussed in detail in Chapter 5.

VISUAL TIME MARKERS

- Use visual timers when the student or classmates find the ring of a regular timer upsetting or disturbing. See Figure 4.7.
- Use a grid to represent time intervals and cross off squares to mark the passage of time.

Labeling

Label objects and centers in the student's environment as much as possible. It encourages prereaders to associate the written word with the object, thus, promoting literacy. Labels also serve to organize the environment; readers find labels especially helpful as they serve as reminders, for example, that books are to be returned to the area labeled "books."

Figure 4.7   The Visual Timer and the Digital Timer

Structuring the Space

Another important environmental consideration is the impact, both positive and negative, that location and space have on the success of students with autism. Keep in mind that some of our students have specific difficulties in planning their movement in space, while others do not automatically pick up the environmental cues of where the activity centers are and the location of supplies. As discussed earlier in the chapter, our students are easily overstimulated and distracted by noise, visual clutter, and lights. Given these factors, we need to ensure that the location of a student's desk in the room minimizes outside distractions as well as distractions from other students, teachers, and even materials; facilitates easy transitions from activity to activity; and brings into focus visual cues that help identify materials, schedules, activity location, and so on. When looking at organizing the space in your room, you will want to consider issues related to the general space and those related to a student's personal workspace. Regarding the general space, one of the first things you might want to consider is the overall layout of your classroom. We would recommend that your room include an individual instruction area and, if possible, a recreational/break/calm down area. Ensure that these locations are clearly marked and visually recognizable by using furniture arrangement and labels. Here are some other issues to keep in mind when structuring space.

INDIVIDUAL INSTRUCTION AREA

An individual instruction area should be placed in the back of a room to minimize distractions and away from a main traffic zone.

- The materials your student needs should be placed in close proximity on shelves to his or her left and marked with a sign, such as work tasks. In front of the student, design a place for work area and to the right a finished area with a container or a shelf for placing the completed work (remember to use a work schedule as described above).
- A student's work place should be clear of clutter.
- Materials should be ready for use before your student sits down.

HOME BASE

Students with ASD benefit from having a home base location in school. Some students need to leave the classroom and go to some other location to either finish their work in a quieter environment or with more one-on-one assistance; others simply need a break from the demands of the classroom; while others may need a safe place to either vent their feelings or calm down after a stressful event. A student's home base is often in the special education resource room; there should be an area designated for the student, such as a study carrel where he or she can go and be alone, with a teacher or paraeducator available for support if needed. This is not a punishment area but a place where the student can gain composure or be successful in completing tasks.

PLACEMENT OF VISUAL SUPPORTS

- *The schedule*—To facilitate smooth transitions, a fixed schedule should be placed at an easily accessible location.
- *The bathroom icon*—If a student needs to request to use the bathroom using an icon, it should be placed by the classroom's door or by the door closest to the bathroom.
- *The break icon*—If a student uses the break icon to request a break from an activity, this icon should be placed at each and every location a student works and within easy reach.

SEATING

- Ensure the student with autism sits comfortably with his or her feet touching the floor and the table is at an appropriate height.
- Ensure that the student's sitting in relation to you encourages good eye contact. If you have a young student in the first days of learning to learn, place his or her chair close enough to allow you to capture him between your legs.
- When the student participates in activities with his or her peers, the student should be seated in the front row as close to the teacher as possible to minimize distractions from other students and to help the teacher utilize the proximity control strategy.
- Sit students with appropriate social skills on either side of your student as good role models and to provide assistance as needed.

MINIMIZE DISTRACTORS

When you interact with the student, it is important to minimize any visual distractions behind you such as busy pictures or a window that reflects too much light.

DISTANCE FROM THE TEACHER

Students with autism are sensitive to personal space, so try to monitor your distance from the student. Sometimes, we have observed that just by moving our chair closer or farther from the student prompted better responses.

PRESENTATION OF MATERIALS

Students with autism are sensitive to how materials are presented. We know, for example, that often students may fail to respond correctly because of the manner in which materials are presented. The most common difficulties students with ASD experience are not knowing what is expected of them and finding the amount presented to be overwhelming. Therefore, break down tasks into manageable units and clearly state what the student is to do with the material.

Structuring the Time

When structuring a student's day, we try to ensure that (a) the curriculum covers all areas necessary for our student's growth; (b) that there is a healthy balance between independent, group, and direct instruction work; and (c) that we are encouraging independence. To accomplish these goals, here are a number of good practice strategies.

What to Do

- Consider the Premark principle when planning your student's time. This principle states that a nonpreferred activity followed by a preferred activity increases the likelihood that the nonpreferred activity is performed more willingly. So we make sure that an activity our student dislikes, such as reading, is followed by an activity he or she looks forward to, such as math.
- Allow the student to choose the order in which various tasks are done during a work session. A detailed discussion of how to use a work schedule to accomplish this is provided on page 40.
- Allow your students to take frequent breaks; they do not need to be long. Be sensitive to their body language and performance so that you may be able to offer a break before your student falls apart. Even better, teach your student to request breaks rather than stop sessions through inappropriate behaviors.
- End your work session on a positive note to increase the probability of compliance for the remainder of the day.
- Do not look at time as a fixed entity. Try to be flexible and responsive to your student's mood and ability to perform on a specific day or time of the day.
- Try to make the preferred activity somewhat longer than the disliked one.
- Use a timer to give your student an advanced warning that a preferred activity is going to end.

Sensory Issues

Today, there is an increased awareness that the sensory system plays an important role in an individual's ability to interact with the environment.

Because we all use our senses to learn about our environment, when the sensory system malfunctions, we are left disoriented, unable to function adequately. A person with ASD might suffer varying degrees of impairments with either heightened or undersensitivity in any one of the sensory systems: gustatory, auditory, visual, tactile, olfactory, proprioceptive, and vestibular (Greenspan & Wieder, 2000). In this section we will discuss the difficulties students with ASD have in each area, and we will also offer some examples of how you can use sensory activities to either calm or alert the student (Anderson, 1998; Kashman & Mora, 2005).

GUSTATORY SYSTEM

It is common to refer to individuals with ASD as picky eaters because they often eat only a limited number of foods. It is not unusual for our students to eat the same lunch, such as a peanut butter sandwich, every day. The limited choice in food is not due to taste only, but it can be caused by its appearance and by its texture as well, as Luke Jackson (2002), an adolescent with AS, explains in his book, *Freaks, Geeks and Asperger Syndrome: A User Guide to Adolescence*, "I don't think the food problems that many autistic and AS kids have are due to them disliking the taste as most won't even try new things. It has to do with the presentation, the texture, and the smell of food as well as them needing sameness" (p. 75).

Remember: Teaching students with ASD to try new foods is a skill that needs to be taught in the same manner we approach teaching new skills in general: planning for it carefully and teaching it gradually. In addition, using a visual aid such as the card illustrated here might also be helpful.

First _____

(Using Velcro, insert either word or picture.)

Then _____

(Using Velcro, insert either word or picture.)

What to Do

Make increasing the variety of foods that students eat one of the curriculum goals. The teaching process includes the following steps:

1. Place a bite of the undesirable food on the plate.

2. Place several bites of the desirable food on a separate plate in plain view.

3. Say, "First (name of undesirable food), then (name of desired food)" while pointing at them.

4. In the beginning, reinforce each bite of the undesirable food with a bite from the desirable food. Gradually, increase the number of bites from the undesirable food before offering one from the desirable kind.

Oral Motor Input and the Gustatory Sense

Calming activities: Chewing gum, licking a sucker, chewing on Thera-Tubing or a stiff straw, and drinking warm liquids.

Alerting activities: Eating foods that are crunchy, salty, chewy, sour, or cold, or drinking cold liquids.

AUDITORY SENSE

As in the case of other sensory modalities, your student can experience auditory difficulties on the entire spectrum, from under (hypo) to extreme (hyper) sensitivity, to certain sounds: sudden sharp noises, specific pitch, and certain sound frequencies, which might explain their sensitivity to selective sounds. Donna Williams (1995) explains this in her autobiography *Somebody Somewhere*: "My father's girlfriend had a high-pitched voice that hurt my ears" (p. 44).

What to Do

- If possible, prepare your student in advance when there is a fire drill in your school.
- During assemblies, and in other noisy environments, provide the student with ear mufflers to block the noise or ear phones to listen to calming music.
- Allow the student to excuse him- or herself from environments that are too painful for him or her, and teach the proper way to do so.
- Make an unpleasant situation predictable through social scripts that explain the situation in advance along with the expected appropriate social behavior.

Auditory Sense

Calming activities: Talk to your student quietly with an even tone, play quiet soothing music, or provide headphones to block out background noises.

Alerting activities: Use an excited voice, vary your pitch and loudness level, or play upbeat music.

VISUAL SENSE

Students with ASD process information through the visual modality easier than through the auditory one. As mentioned above, unlike auditory information, visual aids are static, allowing a student extra time to process information.

Some students engage in stereotyped and repetitive movements (e.g., playing with light and reflections and filtering light through fingers) or unusual visual gaze behavior (e.g., moving close to objects), and may be sensitive to the flicker in fluorescent lighting. Others are distracted by a minute and insignificant object or action (e.g., a tiny mark on a paper, or by a teacher tapping or fidgeting with a pencil).

Remember: Include your occupational therapist (OT) in the discussions of how to provide helpful supports for your student, and ask if there are any sensory strategies that may be helpful.

What to Do

- Use strategies that make information salient such as increasing the contrast of images on pictures or word icons and by using a highlighter to mark the important information.
- Implement the strategies listed at the beginning of this chapter under visual aids.

Visual Sense

Calming activities: Use natural light, dim or turn off the lights, place tissue paper on the cover of fluorescent lights to dull the glare, or allow your students to wear sunglasses; use bland-colored study carrels or dividers to provide a visually distraction free area.

Alerting activities: Use bright lights and bright colors on the walls or on bulletin boards, and use boldly colored materials.

TACTILE SENSE

The sense of touch is essential for normal social and emotional development, and it is crucial in facilitating bonding between child and parents. Often, though, our students with ASD avoid touching new textures or may show great discomfort when being touched. These sensory difficulties are sometimes referred to as tactile defensiveness. As a result of tactile defensiveness, some may become fearful of ordinary daily experiences, such as haircuts, combing hair, cutting nails, and getting dressed. Some are extremely bothered by seams, tags on shirts, or tight waist bands. Wearing new clothes or even sleeping in new sheets may cause some discomfort. In the classroom, students with tactile defensiveness can sometimes be observed to only use their fingertips when playing with materials such as sand, glue, or paint. Others might even withdraw from an activity altogether. Consequently, tactile defensiveness might become a barrier for students in their attempt to learn from their environment.

What to Do

- Plan on teaching your student to gradually tolerate touch of new textures, new materials, new foods, and so forth.
- In some situations, accepting a student's preferences is the right thing to do. Cutting a shirt's tag, for example, may be easier than trying to teach a student to tolerate the scratching feeling.
- Use social scripts to make a situation more predictable.
- Use reinforcers to teach tolerance for unpleasant events.
- Pair an unpleasant event with a calming activity. For example, while your student is working on an art project that involves touching an unpleasant material, he or she may be listening to calming music.

Tactile Sense

Calming activities: Receiving deep pressure, such as a back rub, using weighted lap bags, blankets or vests, wearing tight stretchy clothes or a pressure vest, wiggling through a material tunnel or resting between heavy pillows.

Alerting activities: Receiving a light touch to the palm or touching something very cold.

Fidget items can both calm and alert a student.

OLFACTORY SENSE

Many of our students on the spectrum have shared that they experience extreme sensitivity to smells. Hypersensitivity to odors is another factor that might contribute to a student's avoidance of new foods and avoidance of using various materials, such as glue. Therefore, some may stay away from cafeterias, restaurants, or shopping centers where they feel overwhelmed by the overpowering smells. "I still cannot bear to go past fish shops and the smell of strong perfumes makes me sneeze" (Jackson, 2002, p. 75), says Luke, an adolescent with AS.

What to Do

- In some situations, respecting a student's preferences is the right thing to do, as some may experience extreme allergic reaction to some odors.
- If possible, plan to desensitize your student gradually so that he can slowly start to enjoy and to benefit from his surroundings.

- Pair an unpleasant event with a calming activity. For example, while your student is in the cafeteria, he may be listening to calming music or wearing a weighted vest.
- Allow your student to have control over his environment by teaching him appropriate ways to request permission to leave an unpleasant location.

Olfactory Sense

Calming activities: Sweet smells.

Alerting activities: Sour smells and strong smells.

Pay attention to the perfumes, deodorants, and lotions that you or others are using and to environmental smells, such as food preparation, because they may be highly distracting or even offensive to your student.

PROPRIOCEPTIVE SENSE

The proprioceptive sense gives us information about how our body moves in space through the use of muscles and joints. An impaired proprioceptive system might affect our ability to carry out tasks that require coordination, such as pouring water from one container to another, getting up out of a chair easily and navigating through a row of desks, as well as fine motor activities, such as handwriting. In fact, many students on the spectrum experience dysgraphia, that is, impairment in handwriting. Some have such illegible handwriting that they cannot use their notes for studying. Others may take a very long time to write a short paragraph. These difficulties may even lead to inappropriate behaviors to get out of completing an assignment.

Because of their impaired proprioceptive system, many of our students may be more impacted by the type of pressure they receive on their body. Some do not want to engage in heavy work tasks while others may seek out sensation by falling off their chairs or bumping into walls or other children. Some report that light pressure creates for them heightened arousal and causes discomfort while deep pressure calms them. "I was one of these pressure seekers. When I was six, I would wrap myself up in blankets and get under sofa cushions because the pressure was relaxing," describes Grandin (1995, p. 62).

Remember: Ask a student's permission before touching him or her or give an advance warning before doing so.

What to Do

- Enlist the help of an OT who can guide the exercises needed to improve fine motor skills.
- Teach your student to use a writer, a small computer that can only be used as a word processor.

Figure 4.8   Weighted Lap Bag

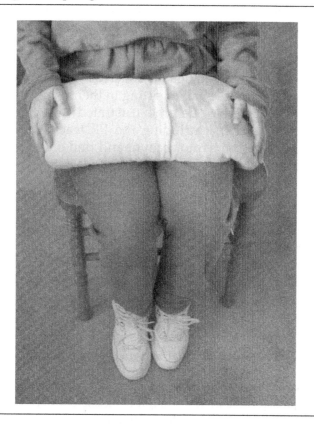

- Modify the amount of work, or the amount of handwriting you require.
- Give your student a written summary of the main ideas to study from and even the daily agenda.
- Provide deep pressure with a weighted lap bag, weighted or pressure vest, wrist and ankle weights (see Figure 4.8) which can be obtained from your OT.
- Avoid patting your student lightly.
- Avoid touching your student without warning.
- Teach your student to communicate the type of pressure he or she needs using concrete tools, such as the 5-Point Scale.
- Integrate calming and alerting activities based on your student's needs throughout the day.

VESTIBULAR SENSE

The vestibular (movement) system processes information about how the body interacts with gravity as it moves and maintains its balance. This system is located in the inner ear, and it gives people information on their body positioning relative to the ground even when their eyes are closed. The vestibular system allows a person, for example, to sit upright in a chair. In people with ASD, this system can be impaired, and it can affect our students in various ways: Some are clumsy; some have poor gross motor skills; others have poor posture or poor balance; and, finally, some have a great need for vestibular input and, therefore, engage in a lot of movement.

There is, therefore, little wonder that many students on the spectrum struggle in PE and in recreational games, such as soccer, baseball, basketball, and even in walking down the hall or sitting in their chairs during class. In all of these situations, they may become frustrated and have inappropriate behaviors. Informed teachers, including the PE teacher, who are aware of these characteristics take them into account and find alternative ways to help students with ASD be successful in their activities.

What to Do

- Make sure your student can sit comfortably in his chair, with feet touching the floor.
- Consider also providing a T-stool or a therapy ball for the student to sit on.
- Encourage the student to use the playground equipment since swinging and climbing will promote vestibular development.

Proprioceptive System and Vestibular System

Calming activities: Carrying and pushing heavy objects, such as carrying books to the library, moving chairs, or pushing the lunch cart; swinging or rocking and other slow, rhythmic gross motor activities, such as bouncing on a therapy ball or jumping on a trampoline; pushing against a Thera-Band wrapped around the legs of the chair.

Alerting activities: Jumping on a trampoline, sitting on a ball rather than on a chair, taking a quick walk down to the office to deliver a message, bouncing on a therapy ball, jumping, dancing, running, or climbing on playground equipment.

In conclusion, many students with ASD struggle to process and to gain useful meaning from the information they receive through their senses. Often, their sensory system is a barrier to their ability to participate in and to learn from their environment. Remember Mike from our vignette? In view of the information provided in this chapter, how would you handle the situation if you were his teacher? A simple approach would be to find out from Mike what it is about the assembly that bothers him—the noise, the crowdedness, the sitting location, the closed room, and so forth. Based on his answers, we would devise corresponding supports, such as allowing him to sit at the edge of a bench and freedom to leave the room when the commotion gets too much for him to handle. We would also, of course, ensure that all teachers who work with Mike are aware of these accommodations. Whatever the needs may be, the main point to remember is that a carefully crafted individualized education plan (IEP) should also include supports that take into account a student's unique sensory profile.

5

Choosing the Interventions

Dan, who has autism, is in middle school and participates in all general education classes. In some classes, he performs fairly well, while in others, such as English, he has failing grades. Dan's English teacher reports that the main problem is that he does not hand in assignments.

His teachers are also concerned that Dan keeps peeling the skin off his hands. One teacher explains, "I've repeatedly told Dan to stop. I've even asked him several times why he keeps doing this, but he can't seem to tell me." And, in general, Dan's teachers note that whenever they ask him a question, he always takes a long time to answer.

In this chapter we discuss specific interventions that we have found effective in our work with students with autism spectrum disorder (ASD), with a focus on those that can be easily implemented in the general education classroom. This chapter covers interventions in four major areas: academics, behavior, communication, and social. A special section is also devoted to applied behavior analysis (ABA) because its principles provide the foundation for many strategies that we discuss, and we also describe what an ABA program would look like in the school setting.

Academics

As discussed in Chapter 1, students with ASD may be found at any point on the continuum of abilities, from those with mental retardation to those with average and even superior abilities. Despite this wide range, a number of strategies have been found helpful for many students on the spectrum. This section addresses the interventions that help them succeed in their general education curriculum while working side by side with their peers.

THE VISUAL TRANSITION SCHEDULE

As already mentioned in previous chapters, a visual schedule is a crucial support for many students. Once the visual schedule is developed, make sure the student is taught how to use it and then expected to use it regularly, until it becomes integral to his or her routines. A common complaint is that "John has a schedule, but he's not using it." However, this is probably because John was not taught how to use it. It is part of our responsibility to both teach John how to use a schedule and to ensure that he does so consistently.

Another common question is, "Should Danielle have a schedule even though she transitions well from one place to another?" Although a student may transition easily from one activity to another, a schedule can help us communicate to him or her when there is a change in schedule. Additionally, for our students on the spectrum we are concerned with their long term independence and the sense of security that a schedule provides.

THE PARAEDUCATOR IN YOUR CLASS

Paraeducators frequently play a crucial role in the successful inclusion of students with autism into the general education classroom. However, it is important that you continue to be the student's main teacher. If your student does not readily follow the directions given to the entire class, address the student by name and give the instructions individually. Make every effort to teach your student to pay attention to *you*, rather than to become dependent on a paraeducator's prompt. Here are some strategies to accomplish this:

- During whole classroom instruction, keep the verbal interaction between the paraeducator and the student to a minimum.
- If a student has difficulty in following an instruction, the best way for a paraeducator to provide help is often through physical assistance from behind.
- If a student who can read has trouble remembering all the steps of an instruction, the paraeducator can write them down for him.
- If the student is a nonreader, the paraeducator can reiterate the instructions one step at a time.

Finally, where paraeducators sit or stand can be a crucial factor in promoting students' learning and independence. For example, when paraeducators position their bodies in a certain way, they can steer students in the right direction. They must also be careful not to block the student from seeing the teacher and avoid becoming a barrier between the student and the materials or between the student and the peers. In fact, the more the paraeducator can be seen as a support to all students, assisting them both academically and socially, the easier it will be for the paraeducator to help integrate the student with autism into a wide range of learning activities (Simpson, de Boer-Ott, & Myles, 2003). Paraeducators can then take the lead by encouraging, modeling, and prompting social exchanges between students with autism and their peers (Koegel, et al., 2006).

INDEPENDENT WORK STRATEGY

Many of our students have difficulty getting started on their work and completing it. This can be caused by anxiety that the work is too hard for them and that they might make mistakes, or fear that the assignment will take forever to complete, and sometimes having difficulty planning where or how to start. Some students need constant reassurance that what they are doing is fine. Below are some ideas we found helpful in alleviating students' anxiety and increasing their independence.

- Provide students with written guidelines, such as the checklist in Figure 5.1, to help them remember where and how to start. This card will typically be laminated, and students will be provided with an erasable marker to checkmark the items as they perform them. When the assignment is complete, an adult will ensure that this checklist is cleaned and ready for the next time it is needed. Again, for this tool to be effective, students need to be taught how to use it.

Figure 5.1   Checklist for Starting an Assignment

To start an assignment, I need to do the following:

❑ Get out my pencil.

❑ Write down my name.

❑ Read and answer the questions.

❑ When finished, hand it in to the teacher.

- Provide a slight touch from behind.
- Put your hand on the student's hand to direct him or her to hold the pencil.
- Point to the location on the page where the writing needs to begin.
- Highlight the location on a page where the student should start writing.
- Structure the work environment. Design start, work, and finish areas for completing assignments. Place the assignment in a start container

which can be in the form of a box for a younger student (see Figure 5.2) or a folder for an older one (see Figure 5.3). The start folder is placed on the student's left-hand side. On his right-hand side, place the finish container. Teach the student to take the assignment from the left-hand side folder (the start folder) and to put it in front of him or her to work on it. Once the assignment is completed, teach the student to place it in

Figure 5.2 Treatment and Education of Autistic and Related Communication-Handicapped Children (TEACCH) Layout for a Young Student

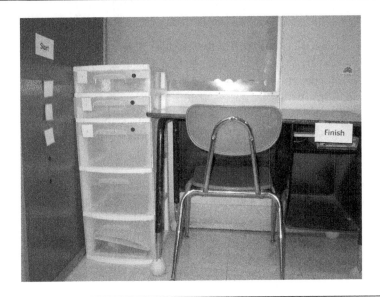

Figure 5.3 Treatment and Education of Autistic and Related Communication-Handicapped Children (TEACCH) Layout for an Older Student

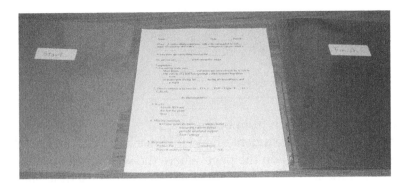

the finished folder. When all assignments on the left-hand side have moved to the right-hand side, students know that they are done and can choose a reinforcer. The teaching of this system is done through gradual guidance from behind. This system was developed by the Treatment and Education of Autistic and related Communication-Handicapped Children (TEACCH) at the University of North Carolina.

- The first . . . then . . . strategy (see page 48) works like magic for many students. On the back of the *first . . . then . . .* card place icons of your student's reinforcers. Start work by asking, "What would you like to work for?" while showing your student the menu of reinforcers at the back of the card. For younger students or for those who are just learning the system, provide the reinforcer immediately upon work completion. Start by ensuring the student's success with small amounts of work and gradually increase expectations.

- Shorten assignments. If students can show that they understand a concept after completing only 10 problems, consider cutting down on the number of problems. When shortening an assignment, present only the required work on a page rather than just crossing out the extra portion. A visually busy page can be stressful, even if we tell the student to answer only the first three questions or only the odd numbers.

- An assignment that is given in the form of a long project provides unique challenges. So break it down into small parts and assign a deadline for each part—something like a minischedule for the entire project. Allow your student to hand in each part as it gets completed to ensure that it does not get lost.

- For students who find it difficult to write even a short paragraph, number the amount of lines or sentences you expect them to write, or draw the number of lines needed to be filled in order to complete the assignment.

- Incorporating choice making can increase motivation and ownership of an assignment. Choice making can be done in several forms:
  o Give the student a choice of two or three different assignments on the same topic/skill.
  o Give the student a choice on how to write the assignments—using a pencil, scribe, or computer.

- Incorporating a student's obsession or topic of interest in the assignment also increases motivation. Although this requires some creativity, it is sometimes possible to accomplish; when teaching math, for example, for a student who is interested in airplanes, you might make up problems related to air travel.

- Some students take too long to complete an assignment because they are perfectionists; their letters need to look perfect or they are afraid of making a mistake. If this is the case, write a Social Story that explains that people draw letters differently and this is just fine.

ORGANIZATIONAL ISSUES

A common frustration of teachers is that even when students have completed their assignments, they might not get them turned in. So for many students, our goal is to teach them how to find the assignment in their backpack, to then remember to turn it in, as well as how to distinguish between notes and assignments. If you look in some backpacks, you might think that a whirlwind passed through them. It is, therefore, no wonder that assignments get lost. Below are some strategies that we have found effective for our students:

- *Color-coded folders*: Assign one color of folder for collecting homework (e.g., yellow), another for returning completed assignments (e.g., orange), and a different color for notes or papers to study from for a test (e.g., green). It is helpful to have a routine and a central location for assigning and collecting homework. When establishing this routine, the teacher or a peer can start reminding the student to check his or her yellow or orange folders. When these activities become part of a student's routine, the teacher will gradually be able to fade the reminders. To help the student place papers in the correct folders, mark each paper with a corresponding highlighter.
- *Providing students with a duplicate set of books for use at home*: This will relieve the stress of having to remember which books to bring home every night or to bring back to school.
- *Developing a consistent home-school communication system*: Establish a home-school communication system for parents to stay informed regarding homework requirements, tests, and any other events the student may have difficulty remembering, so they can in turn help their child at home.

Remember: Each student is different, so our challenge is to find the particular system that matches the unique needs and preferences of our students.

One of the major challenges is for students to "buy into" your system. If students think the system is stupid, they will refuse to use it. So for any system to succeed, our students need to feel they own it—a sense that it works for them.

TRANSITIONING TO A NEW TOPIC

Some students have difficulty transitioning from subject to subject. Here are some ideas that can help:

- *Advance warning*: Give students ample advance notice that they will have to stop what they are doing and transition to the next activity. (If advanced warning is not working for your student, it possibly means that stopping an unfinished activity or assignment and moving on to something else may constitute a new skill that your student needs to be taught explicitly.)
- *Priming:* For some students, new material can cause anxiety, which can prevent them from focusing on the teacher's information; for others, the irrelevant details of new material can be distracting. Therefore,

spending a few minutes familiarizing students with the new material ahead of time in a relaxing environment, such as a resource room, can help students focus on the teacher's explanation later on in class (Koegel & Koegel, 2006).

MAINTAINING FOCUS

One of the biggest challenges for our students is maintaining focus while the teacher discusses a topic with the entire class. Some strategies, in addition to priming, that help our students maintain attention are delineated below:

- *Preferential sitting*: Place your student in the middle of the front row to minimize distraction from peers and other activities happening in the classroom.
- *A fidget item*: Some students focus best when they can keep their hands busy holding a fidget item, or running them across a strip of Velcro attached to the desk, or doodling.
- *Short breaks*: Others benefit from taking short breaks. So if you notice that students are becoming disruptive or are not paying attention, why not send them on an errand to the secretary or to the fountain to take a drink.
- *A nonverbal signal*: Another tactic is to use a nonverbal, nonintrusive cue to redirect students, such as tapping on the table or pointing at the book.
- *Small chunks of work:* Cut the work down into smaller amounts, allow students to take frequent short breaks, and provide reinforcers following each chunk of work. Even better, teach them to reinforce themselves upon completion of each segment of the work.

NOTE TAKING

Even high-functioning students with ASD often have difficulties taking notes in class. There are several factors that make note taking so challenging for these students. Some struggle with fine motor activities in general, including handwriting, known as dysgraphia. Others have difficulty pinpointing the main idea that they need to write down. In addition, note taking usually involves listening and writing at the same time and dividing their attention between two different activities is often very difficult for our students. Finally, organizing the information on paper may not be an easy task, and as a result, their notes do not become a helpful study resource. To help with note taking several ideas have been proposed:

- *A full set of notes:* The teacher provides the student with complete notes before each class.
- *The clause format*: The teacher provides the notes but leaves out some key words for the student to fill in while listening. This minimizes the need for writing and encourages the student to focus on the teacher's presentation. For lower functioning students who struggle with writing, consider using sticky labels with the answers already written. The student's task is to find the correct word and put it in the right spot (see Figure 5.4).

- *A scribe*: The paraprofessional could serve as the student's scribe and provide the notes.
- *A peer's carbon copy notes*: Another student could provide a copy of his or her own notes.

Figure 5.4   A Note-Taking Strategy

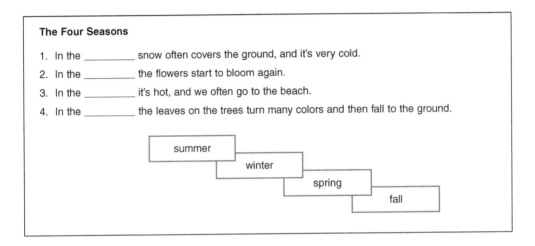

RUSHING THROUGH WORK

If you have students who complete their work poorly because they are intent on getting it done fast, use the visual strategy in Figure 5.5 to help slow them down and to focus on accuracy.

Figure 5.5   Strategy for Slowing Down and for Improving Work Accuracy

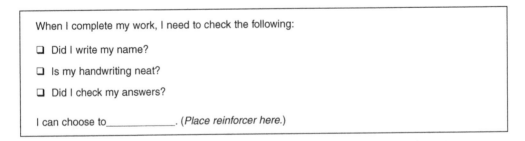

**ASKING TOO MANY QUESTIONS
AND MAKING IRRELEVANT COMMENTS**

Tell students who ask too many questions or make irrelevant comments that they are allowed to ask (or make comments) only a certain number of times during a lesson. Count every time they ask a question, reminding them of the number of questions that are still left to use. You may even provide concrete visuals for them to use each time they ask something, such as question cards (see Figure 5.6). You may start, for example, by giving students four cards to use, and every time they ask a question, they give their teacher a question card. When all the cards are gone, they will know that they cannot ask any more questions.

Figure 5.6   Strategy for Limiting the Number of Questions

DIFFICULTY UNDERSTANDING NEW CONCEPTS

If you have students who take longer than their peers to process new information, you may use the following strategies:

- *Priming:* Use this strategy to familiarize the student with the concept ahead of time, before it is presented in class.
- *Direct instruction:* Your student may need more intensive teaching to practice a specific skill. This can be accomplished in a one-on-one setting with the resource room teacher or paraeducator.

ORGANIZING INFORMATION AND THOUGHTS

Students with ASD often struggle to organize all the information they receive in their classes. Even those students who are able to learn new material with ease find it difficult to organize their knowledge for discussions or report writing. Additionally, unable to sort the information, or to make inferences, or even to have an opinion, or come to a conclusion, they may fail to see *the forest for the trees*. Various teaching tools that allow the student to see a visual organization of the information are very helpful. In particular, outlines and graphic organizers of all sorts have been used successfully to create a concrete mental picture of the concept including the following:

- Inspiration software makes using graphic organizers fun and easy and can be found at http://www.inspiration.com/.
- KWL, an acronym for What we *K*now, What we *W*ant to Know, and What we *L*earned, encourages active thinking during reading. Each student is given a chart with three columns, titled K, W, and L, and they are asked to fill in both the K (what we know) and the W (what we want to know) before they begin reading. After reading, they fill in the L (what we learned) column. It serves to motivate the students to think about the subject matter, organize their thoughts, and engage them in the process of reading to gain information (Ogle, 1986; see Figure 5.7).

Figure 5.7   What We Know, What We Want to Know, and What We Learned (KWL)

What We Know	What We Want to Know	What We Learned
Cats have kittens.	How many kittens can they have?	Cats are called felines.
Mother cats take good care of their kittens.	What does it mean to say that they have nine lives?	They can walk along narrow edges without falling.
Lions and tigers are big cats.	How many different kinds of big cats are there?	Cats can live in places that are very cold and places that are very hot.

Many other organizers are available commercially and also free over the internet to assist with storytelling, sequencing, categorization, comparing and contrasting, as well as hypothesizing and brainstorming.

UNDERSTANDING ASSIGNMENT EXPECTATIONS

Understanding the teacher's expectations for an assignment can be particularly problematic for students with ASD. Here are some ideas for you to try out:

- *Examples:* Provide an example of the assignment. If, for example, you want students to show their work in math, provide an example that delineates the exact steps that they need to follow for each problem.
- *Written instructions*: When an assignment is to write a paper on a certain topic, provide written instructions on how many paragraphs you want, what should be discussed in each paragraph, and, if possible, provide an example of a finished paper.
- *From abstract to concrete:* Our instructions are often not followed because they are too abstract. For example, Ms. Raines told her class, "Please, write what you want to be when you grow up," and she even provided examples. Rob did his best, but not knowing where to start, he wrote something that was

completely irrelevant. To get him to think again about the question, the teacher asked him what he liked to do at home, and the student responded, "play video games." Their discussion was the support he needed; it led him to consider becoming a videogame designer one day, and now, he was relieved to have something to write about.

INCREASING STUDENT PARTICIPATION

Increasing student participation improves learning and a student's self-esteem. Here are some strategies to do so:

- *Ask questions you know the student can answer:* Involve students with ASD in a discussion by asking them a question to which they know the answer, and remember to reinforce them even when you do not reinforce others for the same behavior. If needed, practice with students the answers to several questions related to the topic a day prior to the discussion in class.
- *Index cards:* Provide the student with the written answers on one index card or on separate index cards (Fisher, 2006).

In this section, we discussed strategies commonly used for students with ASD in the general education setting to help them learn the academic content alongside their peers. As we all know, our students' behaviors can often be quite mystifying! We encourage you, therefore, to be creative and on the lookout for innovative strategies.

Behavior

Is your student self-injurious? Is he or she hurting him- or herself, or is he or she sometimes aggressive towards others? Or perhaps your student is noncompliant, often refusing to follow your instructions? If you have answered yes to any of these questions, then this section will be of interest to you. We will start by discussing the assumptions underlying our approach to addressing behaviors. We will then offer specific strategies that we have found effective for students with ASD.

First, we believe in addressing challenging behaviors from a therapeutic rather than a punitive perspective. The assumption is that often students with disabilities do not choose to misbehave; rather, the inappropriate behavior is related to the student's disability. Take, for example, Carla's case: Carla is a third grader with autism who frequently gets up from her desk without permission. If her teacher assumes that Carla behaves this way because she is making a bad choice, the teacher will probably choose a punitive approach. That is, the teacher will punish Carla to teach both her and her peers the consequence for such a behavior. If, however, the teacher assumes that something other than willfulness is causing Carla to want to get up and move about frequently, the teacher will decide to treat this behavior in a therapeutic manner. This means that the teacher will look for ways to either help Carla increase the amount of time that she remains seated or teach Carla appropriate ways to take breaks and return to work. In other words, from a therapeutic perspective, the teacher may well conclude that punishing Carla is not going to teach her to stay in her chair.

In addition, we regard behaviors as communicative. That is, behaviors serve a purpose for the student; they communicate his or her needs or wants. Generally, a behavior serves one or more of the following purposes: requesting an item, avoiding a demand or situation, satisfying a sensory and biological need, or requesting attention. So whenever a student exhibits an inappropriate behavior, first look at what purpose the behavior serves. Once this is determined, the next step is to focus on solutions that consider the root cause of the behavior and teach our student a new socially acceptable behavior to replace the maladaptive one. It is therefore important to keep in mind that the new behavior we teach should fulfill the same function as the old one that is being replaced. If at all possible, it is best to teach a replacement behavior that is incompatible with the maladaptive one. For example, teaching students to sit in their chairs is incompatible with them walking around, or teaching students to hold fidget items while walking in line through the school's halls is incompatible with them running their hand across the walls. This is also known as the fair pair principle that says that a replacement behavior that is incompatible with the maladaptive behavior strengthens the former while weakening and eventually even eliminating the latter (Kaplan & Carter, 1995).

Furthermore, we address students' behaviors today through a proactive rather than a reactive approach. We analyze the students' environment to look for areas that might trigger or provoke maladaptive behaviors. Questions you might ask are do students understand what is expected of them, or do they have a visual schedule? Do they know how to use it so that we can prepare them for an unforeseen change? Are the students' desks placed in a strategic location in class to minimize distractions? Are they seated between quiet, mature peers? Does work expectation match the students' ability?

And finally, as you may remember from Chapter 1, students with ASD may have both behavior excesses, such as obsessive hand washing, or behavior deficits, such as never initiating conversations with peers. When prioritizing which ones to address first, you will want to tackle behavior excesses before addressing behavior deficits because behavior excesses interfere more significantly with students' everyday functioning and may prevent them from learning new skills. It is, for example, difficult to teach students addition if they spend most of the time flapping their hands in front of their eyes.

All educators now need to know what approach to use when addressing disruptive and challenging behaviors in the school setting. The Individuals with Disabilities Education Act (IDEA) states that the student's educational team should consider positive behavioral interventions, strategies, and supports when addressing behaviors that interfere with a student's or peers' education. These strategies are described in detail below.

Positive Behavioral Supports (PBS)

PBS is an approach that can be used to improve the behavior and learning of not only an individual student but can also be used with the whole class or even schoolwide. At the core of PBS is a respect for all students and a focus on improving their quality of life. It assesses the cause of problem behavior through a functional assessment (see description below), then uses this information to remove environmental or biological triggers and to teach new skills. It does not simply focus on a student's maladaptive behavior; it considers the whole student and his or her social community, and teaches both to interact in new ways (Sugai et al., 2000).

One of the first steps in coming to grips with a student's challenging behavior is to conduct a functional assessment of this behavior. This will allow you to determine the likely causes that feed the behavior and to form the basis of your positive behavioral support plan.

FUNCTIONAL ASSESSMENT

A functional assessment may include indirect assessments, direct observation assessments, and a functional analysis. The goal of these assessments is to formulate a hypothesis for the function of the behavior. The hypothesis will contain information on the setting event, the antecedent to the behavior, the behavior itself, and the consequence that follows the behavior. This will then become the basis of the positive intervention strategy you implement later with your student.

Indirect assessments rely on reports from others, such as written reports, data sheets, questionnaires, and interviews with those who know the student best and are witness to the behavior. One such questionnaire is the Motivational Assessment Scale (MAS) (see Figure 5.8) (Durand & Crimmins, 1992) that can be purchased by writing to Monaco & Associates Incorporated, 4125 Gage Center Drive, Topeka, KS 66604, by calling the company at 785–272–5501, or you may download it from the Web at http://www .monacoassociates.com/mas/MAS.html.

Another useful instrument is the Functional Analysis Screening Tool (FAST) (Goh, Iwata, & DeLeon, 2002), which you can find in Resource H and reproduce to use for your students.

Figure 5.8   The Motivational Assessment Scale (MAS)

Motivation Assessment Scale
By V. Mark Durand and Daniel Crimmins

Name _Johnathan_   Today's Date _8/29/08_

Rater _____Dan_____

Behavior Description _Hand biting - anytime his teeth_
touch his hand

ITEM			RESPONSE				
	Never	Almost Never	Seldom	Half the Time	Usually	Almost Always	Always
1. Would the behavior occur continuously, over and over, if this person was left alone for long periods of time? (For example, several hours.)	0	(1)	2	3	4	5	6
2. Does the behavior occur following a request to perform a difficult task?	0	1	2	3	(4)	5	6
15. Does this person seem to do the behavior to get you to spend some time with him or her?	0	1	(2)	3	4	5	6
16. Does this behavior seem to occur when this person has been told that he or she can't do something he or she had wanted to do?	0	1	2	3	4	(5)	6

SCORING

	Sensory	Escape	Attention	Tangible
Total Score =	4	20	10	15
Mean Score=	1.00	5.00	2.50	3.75
Relative Ranking =	4	1	3	2

monaco
associates

Copyright 1992
1-800-798-1309   www.monacoassociates.com

Source: V. M. Durand & D. Crimmins, *Motivation Assessment Scale (MAS)* (Topeka, KS: Monaco, 1992). Reprinted with permission.

Direct methods of assessment involve observing the student while engaged in the problem behavior as well as observing what else occurs in the environment both before and after the behavior. This can be achieved either through live observation or by videotaping. Data can be recorded as a continuous behavior using forms such as the Antecedent-Behavior-Consequence (A-B-C) form (see Figure 5.9) or by time-sampling or interval-recording methods

Figure 5.9   Behavior Data Form

Student's Name: _____

Data Collectors' Name(s): _____

Behavior: _____ (the behavior must be measurable)

Date	Duration	Frequency	Setting/Activity	Antecedent	Consequences
	Start: _____ End: _____				
	Start: _____ End: _____				
	Start: _____ End: _____				

(see Figure 5.10). A reproducible A-B-C form can be found in Resource E. You can find a more detailed description of how to collect data on a student's behavior in the discussion on ABA, later in this chapter.

Another form of functional assessment, and the most thorough, is a functional analysis which can be conducted to confirm a hypothesis by directly manipulating environmental conditions. For example, Dan, a 10-year-old with autism, used to call out to the teacher or make loud comments, thus frequently disrupting a lesson. The teacher hypothesized that the function of this behavior was to get her attention. To test this hypothesis, the teacher started to systematically provide or withdraw her attention in response to the student's call-outs.

Figure 5.10   Time Sampling Recording

2 min.	4 min.	6 min.	8 min.	10 min.	12 min.	14 min.	16 min.	18 min.	20 min.
−	+	−	+	+	−	−	+	−	−

− indicates off-task behavior
+ indicates on-task behavior

A functional assessment includes the following steps:

- Define the problematic behavior:
  - Describe the maladaptive behavior in observable and measurable terms.
  - Describe the behavior clearly enough that a person who is not familiar with the student can recognize it—the stranger test.
- Choose a data collection system: The recording system you choose will depend on the behavior you want to target. Remember that the system you use to take baseline data will be the same as the one you will use during the intervention phase. See a detailed discussion on the various data collection systems in the section on ABA later in this chapter.
- Collect the following information on the behavior:
  - The number of times the inappropriate behavior occurs
  - The location(s) in which the behavior occurs
  - Under what circumstances the behavior occurs: What precipitates the behavior (antecedent), who is present, what is the activity the student is engaged in when this behavior occurs, what consequences follow the behavior, including how others react, and ecological factors such as weather changes, health changes, and so on. This baseline data on behavior needs to be collected for at least three consecutive days.
- If your assessment includes a functional analysis, you will manipulate the antecedents or the consequences to test the hypothesis, while continuing to take data on the behavior.

It is vital to understand the function of a behavior so that we do not choose interventions that inadvertently maintain the inappropriate behavior. Table 5.1 shows how the intervention we choose is determined by the function of the behavior.

Table 5.1 The Relationship Between the Function of a Behavior and an Intervention

Behavior	Function	Intervention
A student grabbing peers' pencils and mouthing them.	Sensory	Provide for sensory needs: Offer a chewy.
	Avoidance	Do not allow escape; keep student on task.
	Attention	Do not comment on the behavior; rather redirect student to task at hand; reinforce appropriate behaviors.
	Requesting (tangible)	Do not allow access to items; teach appropriate ways to request.

Upon completion of the functional assessment, the next step is to write a PBS plan for your student. The information you gained from your assessment will help you to determine what environmental changes to make and what new skills to teach. Often a student's behavior serves more than one function, and there may be more than one behavior that needs to be addressed simultaneously. So come together as a team to discuss and select the changes and interventions that are appropriate, commit them to writing, and then continue to monitor the changes.

WRITING A BEHAVIOR INTERVENTION PLAN (BIP)

On occasion your student's positive behavior supports may also include a BIP (see Figure 5.11). Whether you are writing a comprehensive PBS or just a BIP, make sure to conduct a functional behavior assessment first to determine the function of the behavior as described above. Here are the steps for writing a BIP:

- Describe the replacement behavior that your student will learn, including the baseline data. Make sure that your description includes the situation under which the behavior will occur.
- Describe the behavior in positive terms. In other words, remember the dead man rule: If a dead man can perform the target behavior as it is stated, the statement needs to be reworded. For example, a statement such as "The student will not shout out" represents an activity that even a dead man can perform, and therefore, it is not appropriate. Rather, reword the description to say something like, "The student will raise his or her hand to request permission to talk." You will then collect baseline data on how often this student raises his or her hand to get permission to talk.
- Ensure that the replacement behavior you choose to teach relates to the function of the behavior (see Table 5.1).
- Describe the intervention procedures in detail so they are clear to everyone working with the student, including a description of any environmental changes that are needed.
- Describe what consequences should follow the student's behavior: What should the teacher's response be if the student fails to respond correctly, and how should the teacher respond when the student is successful?
- Determine the criterion for mastery of the skill that you are working on. With some behaviors, such as biting, your goal will be to reduce the number of incidences to zero. With other behaviors, such as on-task behavior during science class, you will need to know what is considered acceptable and typical behavior. You can determine this by taking data on two or three peers, and then use this as your criterion. Generally,

however, when teaching a new skill, 80% or more on three consecutive sessions is considered mastery. Other factors to consider when you get ready to collect data on behavior are discussed in the section on ABA later in this chapter.

- Decide how often the team will meet to monitor progress and to decide whether the BIP needs tweaking.

Figure 5.11   A Sample of a Behavioral Intervention Plan (BIP)

Date: 03/08/2007

Student Name: Lia Castello

Main Implementer: Ms. Sharp

Behavior	Expected Outcome(s) and Goal(s)	Intervention(s)	Implementers	Intervention Review
Lia refuses to complete assignments in American history. Currently, she completes an average of 58% of the assignments over four consecutive data collection days. Lia often complains that assignments are either too easy or too difficult.	Lia will increase completion of assignments in American history from an average of 58% to an average of 85% in four consecutive data collection days.	Teacher will break the assignments into smaller chunks. The teacher will put the rating scale at the top of her assignments and Lia will mark the level of difficulty. A model of what is expected will be available. A paraeducator will assist Lia to get organized, to work on assignments, and will redirect her if off task. Lia will spend 30 minutes a day in the resource room to work on her American history assignments. She will be given a complete set of notes. Teacher will offer higher-level memorization tasks, to ensure that Lia does not feel the assignment is too easy. If work is completed, Lia will gain access to a reinforcer of her choice. If not completed, Lia will stay after school for 30 minutes once a week to work on assignments.	Classroom teachers or classroom paraeducators.	Weekly

Signatures: _____

- Describe any specific considerations to keep in mind, such as changing procedures in unusual circumstances.

A blank form of a BIP can be found in Resource I. Your school may also have other forms of a functional assessment and a BIP that you can use.

Remember: If no change is observed in the behavior in about two weeks, reevaluate the intervention plan.

BEHAVIOR INTERVENTION STRATEGIES

Here is a review of a number of behavior intervention strategies that are used to teach new skills or for replacing maladaptive ones. Some of these interventions are considered positive behavioral strategies, such as differential reinforcement of alternative (DRA) or incompatible (DRI) behaviors, extinction, contingency contracting, modeling, and redirection. Others are considered punitive (behavior reduction procedures–BRPs), such as reprimands, response cost, overcorrection, time-out, and seclusion.

- *DRA* or *DRI* weakens an unwanted behavior by reinforcing an appropriate one. Whenever possible, the replacement behavior that you choose to teach and the unwanted behavior should be mutually exclusive; that is, the student will not be able to physically engage in both of them at the same time. For example, the student will not be able to comply with a request and refuse to do it at the same time. Therefore, by reinforcing compliance, noncompliant behavior will decrease, because a student cannot perform both activities at the same time. This approach can be used to target a series of inappropriate behaviors, such as sleeping in class, noncompliance, stereotypical behaviors, and more.
- *Extinction* occurs when a behavior is extinguished by eliminating the trigger that maintains the behavior. For example, the most common factor that maintains a behavior in a classroom is attention, either by other students or by the teacher. Remember the example above of the student who used to blurt out questions or comments? The functional assessment of the behavior showed that it was maintained by the teacher's attention. When this attention from the teacher was removed, the behavior decreased. When implementing extinction, remember that it is not uncommon for a behavior to worsen first before improvement occurs. So be patient! On the other hand, because of the potential for a behavior to escalate, you will not want to use this intervention to address aggressive or self-injurious behaviors that can put the student or others in danger.
- *Contingency contracting* is an agreement written by a student and teacher that states the expectations required from the student in order to earn a specific reward.

Figure 5.12   Contingency Mapping

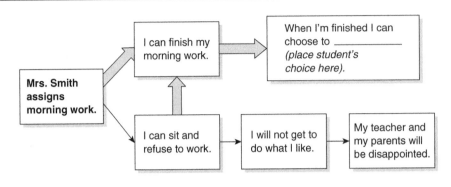

- *Contingency mapping* (see Figure 5.12) involves the use of a graphic representation to show students the consequences of the choices they make. You may use red arrows to signify the wrong path (the thin arrows in the figure) and green ones (the thick arrows in the figure) to signify a correct choice. Make sure to add a green arrow from the wrong choice back to the positive choice, to show that, even when an incorrect choice is made initially, all is not lost and there is a way to make a correction (Brown & Mirenda, 2006).
- *Modeling* is teaching a new skill by showing a student the expected behavior and expecting him or her to imitate it. Modeling is a common technique used to teach social skills in particular. Students typically learn through observation and repeated practices of the skill.
- *Redirection* is the act of refocusing a student's attention on a different task. If, for example, a student is upset because of an argument with a peer, the upset student can be redirected by taking a note to the office.
- *Reduce expectations* on days or times when the student experiences more stress.

Behavior reduction procedures (BRP), as mentioned above, are considered aversive strategies, and they include reprimands, response cost, overcorrection, time-out, and seclusion.

- *Reprimands* involve telling a student that his or her behavior is unacceptable, such as "Please stop talking."
- *Response cost* refers to taking away a privilege as a consequence of an inappropriate behavior. A student, who is trying to win enough tokens to gain access to a reinforcer, may lose one as a consequence of an inappropriate behavior.
- *Overcorrection* involves the restoration of an environment to its initial state or engaging in a repeated practice of a socially acceptable skill that is incompatible with the behavior demonstrated by the student. For example, an overcorrection occurs when a student who ran

halfway down the hall is then asked to walk all the way back to the end of the hall and then back again.

- *Time-out and seclusion* occurs when attention is withdrawn from the student. This can be done by either temporarily withdrawing eye contact (turning your head away), by removing ourselves and others from the student's immediate environment, or by placing the student in isolation. The recommended length of time for seclusion is a maximum of one minute for each year of a student's age. So, a nine-year-old should stay in seclusion no longer than nine minutes. However, be careful because this intervention often backfires with students with autism. Based on what we know about the characteristics of students with ASD (see Chapter 1), students are likely to engage in an inappropriate behavior to escape an unpleasant situation, such as a task that is too difficult or too demanding. So if as a consequence to a maladaptive behavior, we choose to put them in time-out, we are in fact providing the students with the reinforcer that they want, namely getting out of work. The outcome, therefore, will most likely be an increase or maintenance of the inappropriate behavior. Thus, this intervention, like any other, should be considered only as a part of a thoughtful process of a functional behavior assessment (FBA). And finally, remember that a student's maladaptive behavior may be caused by his or her sensory needs (Myles, Cook, Miller, Rinner, & Robbins, 2000) and these must be addressed first.

We strongly encourage the use of positive behavioral strategies that reinforce our students with autism for appropriate behaviors rather than using aversives that punish them for behavioral infractions. However, if you should find yourself in a discussion regarding a punitive strategy, please insist that positive supports also be included. Here are some issues that you should ask everyone to keep in mind before choosing to use punishments as interventions (Alberto & Troutman, 2008; Kaplan & Carter, 1995):

- The intervention should be part of a BIP so that due process is followed and parents' consent is obtained.
- Before using a punishment intervention, demonstrate and document that other positive behavior supports were tried first and failed to produce results.
- The maladaptive behavior you choose to target should have social or academic significance for the student. That is, it should impede his or her functioning socially and/or academically (the behavior should be able to pass the "so what" test).
- Choose the least intrusive or aversive intervention that can achieve the same results.
- Punishments that block a student's access to his or her educational rights, such as extended periods of time-out, should be avoided.
- Continuously monitor the target behavior to document efficacy of intervention.

In conclusion, students with ASD have unique behavioral responses to the demands of their environment. This section offered a description of the interventions that are commonly used for this population to build a new repertoire of skills, to extinguish inappropriate behaviors, and to replace inappropriate behaviors with socially acceptable ones. It also offered a procedure to determine which strategies to implement. Because every student with ASD is unique, interventions need to be tailored to the specific student with whom we are working.

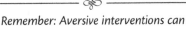

Remember: Aversive interventions can sometimes produce immediate results, but in the long run, they are not as effective in changing behavior.

Communication

As we discussed in Chapter 1, sociocommunicative delays and differences are hallmarks of ASD. While the typically developing student is hardwired for a seemingly effortless acquisition of the language and social behaviors of the surrounding culture, the student with autism often seems like a fish out of water or like someone who has just entered a totally foreign culture. However, because communication and social learning is much more complex than acquiring a simple series of skills in isolation, a multifaceted approach to increasing the sociocommunicative ability of students will be required.

Fortunately, our students with ASD have strengths that we can tap into as we target their communication deficits: Many are visual learners, so make use of pictures or visual representations, exaggerated facial expressions and gestures to supplement the spoken word; many have an excellent rote memory, so take advantage of this by embedding predictable verbal routines into the structure of the day (Cafiero, 1998).

As you select goals and plan interventions, remember that communication is much more than being able to talk; language is the convergence of form, content, and use (Gerber, 2003). Students with ASD must learn about the world around them and gain some understanding of their own feelings and thoughts in order to acquire the words or semantic knowledge of the language. As they acquire the meaning of words, they must also learn the rules or the form of the language, as well as the pragmatics of language use. While it is true that verbal students with ASD may take much longer to learn the form of the language as compared to their peers, this aspect of language acquisition tends, for the most part, to follow the usual developmental milestones. On the other hand, their use of language and their ability to understand others is not simply delayed, it is markedly different and reflects the basic theory of mind (ToM) difficulties they experience (Tager-Flusberg, 1997).

You will find it necessary to address many, if not all, of the following aspects of communication: (a) comprehension of language (receptive language skills); (b) language production (expressive language skills); (c) conversational skills (e.g., turn taking, topic maintenance); (d) pragmatic skills (e.g., social gaze, eye contact, facial expression, gestures, and body language); (e) prosody or rhythm of speech; (f) reading comprehension; and (g) play and friendship skills.

Once your goals for these areas are selected, you are ready to consider which approach or combination of approaches to intervention might be best.

The Main Approaches

Two well-known approaches to teaching language to students in the autism spectrum are the behavioral approach and the relationship-developmental approach. The classical behavioral approach can be characterized as teacher centered whereas the developmental approach follows the student's lead; while the behavioral approach targets specific skills, the developmental approach focuses on increasing social relatedness. The behavioral approach, although highly effective in teaching concrete aspects of language, is less successful in encouraging the spontaneous back and forth of conversation, and those communication skills so crucial to effective social interaction. Out of this difficulty grew the contemporary behavioral approach which combines the use of core behavioral principles while still focusing on the student's natural environment, functional language, and the student's interests. Because of the complexity of language development with its dependence on social development and because of the differences in the learning styles and ability of students in the spectrum, we draw interventions from across the continuum of behavioral and relationship-developmental approaches (Prizant, Wetherby, & Rydell, 2000; Ogletree & Oren, 1998; Goldstein, 2002).

Language Interventions

In this section we provide guidelines for the following stages of language development:

- The *preverbal student*, who has not yet acquired spoken language nor, perhaps, any functional nonverbal form of communication, such as pointing to a desired item.
- The *beginning language learner*, who understands that words are symbols for things, may have learned some phrases but is still not generating many novel utterances and has poor pragmatic skills.
- The *intermediate language learner*, who is in the process of acquiring a wide vocabulary and is beginning to ask questions and express thoughts in full sentences.
- The *advanced language learner* who has a well-established language base but may continue to have profound difficulties with comprehension of text, abstract language, conversational, play, and friendship skills. This section also addresses the needs of students with Asperger syndrome (AS) who have not experienced delays in the acquisition of language but

who struggle both with the understanding of abstract language and the socially appropriate use of language.

- The *nonverbal student* and the need for functional augmentative and alternative communication (AAC) systems. If students with ASD are to make adequate progress, their language and communication skills must be targeted in all settings and throughout the day. Ideally, all who come into regular contact with the student should also have a clear understanding of the specific communicative goals and the methods being used to address them.

Remember: Intervention strategies described within one section may also apply to students in other stages of sociocommunicative development.

The Preverbal Student

Students at the preverbal stage may have some words in their repertoire but are unable to use them functionally, and they are not initiating any meaningful interaction with others.

UNDERSTANDING OF LANGUAGE

Because these students' comprehension of the spoken word is limited, it is important to communicate in a language they can more easily understand. One way is to draw on their visual skills. Here are some guidelines on how to use visual supports to communicate with students:

- Describe the activities of the day using object or picture schedules (see Figures 4.1 and 4.2) or a picture sequence.
- Cue the beginning and ending of activities through the use of "To Do" and "Finished" stacks, boxes, or labels.
- Use labels and signs to make expectations clear (e.g., a picture of blocks to represent the location where blocks are kept and an international "no" sign on the cupboard door to communicate that it must be kept closed).

Other strategies that help the student begin to make sense of the world include the following (Sussman, 1999):

- Using a calm voice and allowing students ample time to process what has been said.
- Using motherese—the exaggerated tone, facial expression, and emphasis on single words and short phrases mothers use with their preverbal children.
- Signaling the end of an activity by using a timer, a song, a sign or phrase.
- Following students' lead and commenting on activities of their choosing.
- Making sure students are attending to what you are saying before you give an instruction.

- Modeling the behavior required or assisting the student by using a hand-over-hand method.
- Maintaining routines that make students' world predictable (this reduces anxiety and increases the ability to attend and learn language).

LANGUAGE USE

Preverbal students may be silent, or they may use a string of sounds not intended for communication. Additionally, they most likely lack the nonverbal language of point, gestures, and facial expressions with which to demonstrate the social and emotional reciprocity crucial to language development. Therefore at this stage, concentrate on teaching the following:

- Create pleasurable routines where the student's attention is focused on an adult or peers, such as in turn-taking games, where both the student and the communicative partner follow each other's lead. These types of activities increase your student's social and emotional reciprocity and help build the back and forth of communication.
- Teach the student to point to pictures, objects, and people.
- Teach imitation tasks that help students learn to attend to another person, to observe, and to follow another's lead. Follow a discrete trial format initially to establish the behavior. Each episode of gaining the student's attention, asking him or her to imitate, and then following up on his or her response is a sociocommunicative event. It may take beginning learners hundreds of opportunities before they successfully learn to imitate a few simple movements. Teach the motor imitation tasks in the following order (Maurice, Green, & Luce, 1996):
  - Gross motor (e.g., clapping hands, tapping the table, and waving)
  - Fine motor (e.g., pointing with the index finger, tapping thumbs together)
  - Oral motor involved in speech production (e.g., blowing, pursing lips)
  - Combined oral motor movements with a sound production (e.g., "aaaah," "oooooh")

Once students can imitate some sounds, you will require them to at least vocalize before they can access a preferred item. When they can imitate fine motor movements, consider teaching them some common signs, such as go, potty, eat, drink, help, and all done. Stay alert to the opportunities that arise throughout the day to teach communication skills in the natural environment.

Another intervention that follows the student's lead and teaches spontaneous initiation of communication without the prerequisites of imitation is the picture exchange communication system (PECS) strategy.

The Picture Exchange Communication System (PECS)

PECS, developed by Bondy and Frost (1994), has been highly successful in teaching students who have little or no functional communicative ability to communicate effectively with both adults and peers. It is particularly helpful for students with autism because it takes advantage of their superior visual skills by using pictures; it does not require the prerequisites of eye contact or a point, and it is also carefully designed to avoid prompt dependence by teaching spontaneous initiation.

The goal of PECS is for students to communicate to others by handing over a picture or pictures of what they want to say. By teaching skills that are immediately functional, such as requesting a desired item, the barrier caused by lack of motivation to talk is overcome; students quickly learn that their wants will be met when they hand the teacher the picture. Additionally, this system has also often resulted in spontaneous verbalizations.

PECS consists of six stages starting at the one-word level in which the student requests an item by giving the picture of that item to the person with whom he or she is communicating. Then the student learns to combine words by using a sentence strip with an "I want" card and attributes along with the desired item. At the final stage, the student learns to use pictures to comment on his or her environment. We stress the importance of systematically teaching students to use the system. If steps are skipped or if not all the staff buy into this communication system, it is unlikely to be successful (Frost & Bondy, 2002).

The Beginning Language Learner

Beginning language learners understand that they can use words to interact with others, and they are beginning to understand what is said. They can communicate wants and needs with one- or two-word phrases, protest verbally, and answer some yes/no questions. Over all, spontaneous speech may be very limited and prompt dependent, but the base of knowledge is growing.

UNDERSTANDING OF LANGUAGE

It is still important to support the students' understanding of the spoken word through the use of gestures, facial expressions, pictures, icons, and signs. Continue to speak in short, clear sentences allowing time for the student to process what has been said.

The following skills are often learned best through discrete trial teaching (DTT) as described later in the section on Applied Behavior Analysis (ABA). You must then generalize these skills by teaching them throughout the day—at recess, lunch, and in the classroom. Teach them in the order given as follows:

1. Follow one-step instructions, such as "come here," "sit down," "clap hands," and "jump."

2. Identify names of objects. Once students respond correctly to between five to ten one-step instructions, begin to systematically teach them to identify the names of objects. Initially, choose a set of five to ten common nouns, and once these are learned move on to another set of ten concrete objects. You may find that by the time you have taught students to point to objects or pictures of the words you say, they have already mastered the production of these words. Continue to teach vocabulary including verbs, adjectives, and the function of objects, people, and places using both pictures and objects.

Many students with autism are drawn to the alphabet, numbers, and colors and may be able to identify and label these before they are able to understand more functional language such as, "Do you want some juice?" Students may be interested in the written word, and this can be a helpful way to learn that words have specific meanings. Here are some suggestions:

- Place labels on items in the room (e.g., computer, door, desk, plant, and floor).
- Provide an album with pictures of teachers and classmates and include their names.
- When there are choices available within classroom routines, have the written words available for the student to choose from (e.g., line leader, snack helper, art area, and book area).
- Use the written word as a support to teaching vocabulary and sentence structure. This is especially helpful for hyperlexic students who have a precocious ability to read words but great difficulty understanding verbal language.

Continue to use the visual supports listed in the previous section for the preverbal student. Learning language is always dependent on hearing the language spoken. In the case of students with ASD, it is especially important that they can connect what they hear to something concrete. As adults describe what they are doing, seeing, or feeling, they provide a model for the student to follow (Sussman, 2006). Here are some helpful language enhancement techniques that can be used throughout the day:

- *Self-talk*: In self-talk, you describe what you are doing, seeing, or feeling. Carefully choose your words and sentence structure to be as clear as possible to the student who is listening (e.g., "I am opening my book. I am reading a story. I am closing my book. I am finished reading.").
- *Parallel talk:* In parallel talk, you describe what the student is doing, seeing, or feeling. Parallel talk provides the link between language and the world of the student (e.g., "You fell down. Your knee is scraped. You are sad.").

LANGUAGE USE

As students begin to acquire expressive language skills, there is much that can be done throughout the day to assist them in this process. Language development for students with autism may not follow the typical pattern of receptive language preceding expressive language. We have worked with students who when asked to point to or hand us the object we named did not know which one to choose, but they could label all those same objects. This difficulty did not last long but taught us to move on to teaching expressive language even when the comprehension was lagging.

As your students begin to use one-word utterances functionally, begin teaching two-word combinations, short phrases, and then onto sentences. You will want to expand their expressive vocabulary and also encourage use of the pragmatic rules of the language. Here are some guidelines:

- First, teach those words that are most relevant to a student's situation and those which will allow access to those people, places, and things most wanted or needed. So you should first help your student learn to use the words that have functional value and reference things of interest, such as "more," "mom," "outside," "cookie," "water," or "hot dog," rather than insisting on the use of social niceties. Once a student is fluent in two- or three-word combinations, by all means encourage the use of "please," "thank you," and "you're welcome."
- Intensive teaching of expressive vocabulary can be accomplished very well through a DTT format. By initially limiting distractors and presenting an object or pictorial representation of the word, it is clear to the student what specific item the word being taught represents.
- Quickly move to requiring a number of different questions be answered in quick succession. Not only will you ask the name of the object ("What is this?"), but you will also ask for a descriptor ("What color is it?") and its function ("What can it do?"). So you will want to teach adjectives, function of objects and body parts, categorization, pronouns, possession, as well as how to protest and answer yes/no questions (Sundberg & Partington, 1998).

MAKING CHOICES

At this stage many students, when asked to make a choice, will respond by repeating the last thing you offer. For example, when asking students, "Do you want to color with a marker or with a crayon?" they are most likely to answer "crayon." You can alternate the order, and if the answer is still "crayon," this is clearly what was wanted. If, however, on the second try the student says "marker," then this is where the visual support (either the actual objects or pictures of them) must be offered to determine the student's preference.

COMMUNICATION TEMPTATIONS

This strategy refers to setting up the environment to entice the student to communicate (Wetherby & Prizant, 1989). You can do this in many different ways:

- Withhold an item needed to engage in an activity (e.g., provide the meal at lunchtime but withhold the utensils; give the paper to write with but not the pencil) so the student has to make a request. This strategy is also known as sabotaging the environment.
- Place a sought after item in a visible but inaccessible location so that the student must request it.
- Engage in a highly preferred activity with the student and then stop abruptly in the middle of it.
- As you sing familiar songs, leave off the last word of each line so the student has an opportunity to sing that word by himself.

JOINT ACTION ROUTINES (JARs)

This is another successful strategy for increasing language abilities in students with autism. It involves student and adult or student and peers interacting in an activity that follows a logical sequence in which each participant plays a recognized role that is essential to the successful completion of that sequence (Snyder-McLean, Solomonson, McLean, & Sack, 1984). There are three main types of JARs: (a) activities associated with a specified end product or outcome (e.g., making a snack); (b) routines developed around an activity story line (e.g., Halloween night); and (c) routines related to cooperative turn-taking (e.g., playing a board game).

JARs are characterized as routines that contain a unifying theme, a joint focus, a limited number of clearly delineated roles, exchangeable roles, and a predictable turn-taking sequence. The advantages of using JARs with students with autism are (a) the routine is comforting, and the predictable sequence and frequent repetition assists in language learning; (b) generalization of language structure and pragmatic skills are encouraged because routines take place in the natural environment; and (c) role reversal allows the student to gain the other person's perspective. Again, remember that language development requires careful planning and practice, practice, and more practice. These are all built into JARs.

LANGUAGE MODELING AND EXPANSION

Using self-talk and parallel talk (see above) will allow you to interact with students who may not speak unless asked a question. Although answering questions is certainly an important skill, do not bombard students with questions but balance questions with descriptive statements about what you are seeing and observing. This is especially important to remember with our students with ASD because they can easily become prompt dependent and end up not speaking unless they are asked a question. There are two other techniques for interacting with students at this stage of development that will continue to encourage them to communicate but will also provide a correct language model for them to follow:

- *Modeling:* When modeling, you provide the student with the correct form of what he or she said (e.g., when student says, "Him falled down," you respond by saying, "*He fell* down"). Make the student aware of the differences by emphasizing the corrections. It is best not to stop students and ask them to repeat the corrected statement when engaged in a conversation with you because this will disrupt the flow of communication. If needed, you can set aside a time just to drill the sentence structure.
- *Expansion:* When using expansion, you provide students with a fuller statement of what they have just said (e.g., student says, "He fell down," and you respond, "Yes, he fell down the stairs").

Here is an example of how Dave's teacher incorporated both modeling and expansion when working with him:

When Dave is looking at a picture of his mom eating cake, he says, "Mom eating." His teacher's response is "Yes, your mom *is* eating," emphasizing is, thus providing a correct model. Then Dave's teacher expands adding, "Your mom is eating *cake*," to which Dave responds, "Mom eating cake." Dave's teacher now follows by saying, "Yes, Mom *is* eating cake."

EYE CONTACT

To obtain eye contact, you can remind the student verbally by saying "Look at me" or "Look at her" and also by using the following strategies:

- Get down to the student's eye level and wait until he or she looks at you.
- Place the desired object at your eye level, and once the student looks up at it (and you), then, and only then, proceed.
- Point to your eyes when you are talking as a cue to the student to look at you.

The Intermediate Language Learner

Language is becoming more sophisticated as students begin to understand and express themselves in complete sentences, and they use words for different functions, such as greetings, protest, commenting, requesting, and answering.

UNDERSTANDING OF LANGUAGE

This is an exciting stage of language development as students begin to really comprehend what is said to them. Some are beginning to develop reading skills. At this point, we recommend that you begin a formal program—one that has plenty of practice. However, be careful not to withdraw icon or picture supports that you have in place just because they can now read—they may still need the simpler and easier form of visual support.

Teach the following skills using DTT and JARs as well as taking advantage of all the natural opportunities that arise both in the structured and less structured activities of the day:

- Gender and pronouns: Before tackling *he* and *she*, make sure your student can distinguish between boy and girl and between man and woman.
- Feelings: Because students may not be able to identify many different feeling states in themselves, start with the most obvious—happy, sad, mad, tired, and sick.
- Prepositions: Teach one preposition at a time using real objects and simple line drawings.
- Opposites: Use real objects as well as pictures.
- People and places: For example, *Pilots* fly planes; planes fly in and out of *airports*. *Farmers* grow crops; they live on *farms*.
- Nonverbal cues: Teach students to pay attention to the speaker and to follow nonverbal cues.

LANGUAGE USE

As mentioned above, sometimes language use will precede the understanding of language in students with ASD. So although they are now using words, phrases, or even whole sentences, they may not truly understand what they are saying and will still benefit from visual supports. For example, some students are echolalic and repeat all or part of a question or statement just made to them, recite sections of movies, conversations heard previously, or even a passage just read, and yet, they do not understand the content of these words.

ECHOLALIA

Many teachers voice concern about what to do when a student's communication is clearly echoic. It is best to view this situation positively because it allows the student to practice spoken language, and it displays a desire on the part of the student to communicate: So accept the echolalic utterance, and use it to encourage further communication as in the example below.

As with immediate echolalic utterances, delayed echolalia can be used to foster further communication. A student I worked with, who repeated many lines from the Cinderella movie, would, whenever she heard my clock striking, repeat the line "Oh, that clock!" with great emphasis. Because this could be used as a springboard for more conversation on what time it was and what we would do next, I did not discourage her from saying it. However, when she would launch into long repetitions of movie lines, I would redirect her to the topic we had been discussing. In other words, accept echolalic utterances when it allows you and your students to enter into a conversation, but when it does not serve a social function, it is best to tell them to stop. The following techniques will help establish the forms and functions of the language:

- Teach students the basic structure of language (e.g., "The big boy sits on the purple chair," "The little dog sleeps under the tree") using DTT, and then provide ample opportunities for generalization throughout the day.
- Teach the pronouns "I" and "you" through pairing a cue card with the correct response.
- Focus on teaching functional carrier phrases throughout the day in all settings:

  "I want the (a) _____."

  "I see the (a) _____."

  "I have the (a) _____."

  So, for example, when walking a student to the bus, you will have the opportunity to say, "I see the bus," "I see the bus driver," and "I see your friend ____." After some days of doing this, you might now say, "I see Susie. Who do you see?" and then encourage the use of the complete "I see _____" sentence for a response.

- Combine the written words with the instructions that you are teaching even if the student is not a reader. For example, when teaching a student the construction "Pronoun–is–verb-ing," point to each word on the cue card in Figure 5.13 as the student learns to imitate your model of the sentence.

Figure 5.13   A Sample of a Cue Card for Teaching Sentence Structure

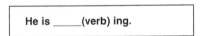

He is _____(verb) ing.

- Throughout the day, keep in mind what your language goals are and create opportunities for practice, as follows:
  o Prepare the environment so that there are opportunities to engage the student in the desired learning.

- Have items of interest to the student at hand to encourage him or her to initiate.
- When you initiate, be sure to get the student's attention before engaging in a language learning opportunity.
- Make sure your language demands are within the student's range.
- Balance easier language demands with more challenging ones.
- Provide immediate positive feedback or model the correct response.
- Practice, practice, practice.

Here is an example of how Ravi's teacher incorporated these guidelines into her student's day.

> Ravi, a first grader who is learning to use pronouns and to speak in complete sentences, has finished his math assignment ahead of time. He is allowed to go to the reading area to look at books until his peers are finished. Ravi's teacher has placed a photo album of him and his peers in that area, and as always, he has chosen to look through it. After a while, the teacher joins Ravi and asks him to show her the album. As they look at the pictures together and talk about them, the teacher encourages Ravi to use pronouns and the present progressive construction. Because he is very secure with the pronoun "he," his teacher first asks what several boys are doing. Once he has had some success, the teacher begins to intersperse the more difficult questions requiring the use of "she." His teacher's goal is to elicit at least 15 to 20 complete sentences. However, she always keeps her tone warm and encouraging; she realizes that building a positive relationship with Ravi will encourage him to initiate future interactions with her.

Further examples and guidelines can be found in the *How to Teach Pivotal Behaviors to Children with Autism: A Training Manual* (Koegel et al., 1989), which can be downloaded at http://www.users.qwest.net/~tbharris/prt.htm.

- Use *scripts* and *script-fading* techniques to help the intermediate language learner acquire a repertoire of basic sentences to use in certain situations (Krantz & McClannahan, 1993). Although a specific dialogue is used, this strategy often results in novel utterances once the student gains confidence in what he or she is communicating. Index cards with written prompts can be used by fluent readers, while a Language Master can facilitate nonreaders to learn their part of the script. The Language Master is an electronic device through which cards with a recordable strip are played. A short message can be recorded on each card and the words or pictures can be added. For example, here is a script used to teach a kindergartener to have a conversation about a weekend activity:

Sam: Hi, what did you do this weekend? (1)

Teacher: I went to Kansas City. What did you do?

Sam: I went to see my grandma. (2)

Teacher: What did you do at Grandma's?

Sam: We went to the park and ate ice cream. (3)

Teacher: Ooh, yum! Where did you go for ice cream?

Sam: We went to Baskin Robbins with my cousins. (4)

Teacher: I like ice cream, especially strawberry ice cream.

Sam: My favorite ice cream is chocolate. (5)

Sam: I like it in a cone. (6)

The script fading technique involves beginning to delete words starting with the last one, until only the blank card remains as a prompt, and then, after a while, even the blank card can be faded.

GESTURES

You may also have to teach your student the use of gestures that enhance communication. Games such as "I'm thinking of something in this room that is_____ (descriptor), can you guess what it is?" where students need to use a distal point along with the question, "Is it the _____?" are useful for developing joint referencing through pointing. Use of gestures can be taught during the following classroom activities:

- Student practices the come here arm gesture while calling peers in from recess.
- Student is asked to be the line leader and to gesture stop when the class is required to wait.
- Student is taught to nod and shake his or her head to indicate yes and no.
- Student is asked to tell peers to be quiet putting his or her finger to the pursed lips.

As you would expect, when students do not know what to say they may use inappropriate and ineffective methods of communication (e.g., hitting the person standing beside them in line). Recognize that even students that may have known what to say may have been too anxious to remember to use words. When this happens, model for them the words and gestures that will express what they are wanting and then help them practice it over and over again. For example, a student who either just waits looking at the teeter-totter or who goes and pushes one of his or her peers off the equipment needs help learning to appropriately gain the peer's attention and then signal through words and gesture, "I want a turn, please."

The Advanced Language Learner

We now turn our attention to the needs of the advanced language learner who has a well-established language base but may still have profound difficulties with comprehension of text and abstract language, as well as conversational, play, and friendship skills.

UNDERSTANDING OF LANGUAGE

Here are some tips for enhancing students' understanding of language:

- Be straightforward and explicit in your directions. Students with ASD will take you literally when you say, "I am waiting for everyone to hand in their papers." They have just heard that you are waiting and that is fine with them because they have not finished their work. However, what you really meant and what the rest of the class understood was, "Hand in your papers now!"
- If you notice students are not following directions, simply call their name and reiterate what you just said. Students with ASD often do not realize that you are addressing them if you do not call them by name, and may, for that reason, totally ignore directions given to the entire class.
- Because our students understand language literally, they will need to be specifically taught the meaning of metaphors and idioms. They may also require extra time or a fuller explanation to be able to enjoy a joke. You will find that once an idiom, metaphor, or joke is explained, your students relish the newfound knowledge—sharing it with everyone! Of course, you will soon realize that you will also have to teach them when and with whom they may try out their new expressions or jokes. After all, the bus driver may not appreciate being told by a third grader to, "Keep your head on!"

COMPREHENSION OF TEXT

Students with ASD have difficulty with the comprehension of text when more than a few sentences are involved. They may read very well and they may indeed comprehend every word but when asked to describe what they have just read, they have no idea how to respond. Even remembering the details may be very challenging. It appears that they were so focused on the individual words that they did not take in the meaning of the whole. A strategy that helps students understand and retain what they have read is to have them draw pictures of the different scenes as they read through the text, or you can draw with them. The drawing need not be fancy. Just take a regular size piece of paper, fold it in half, and make four boxes on each half of the paper that you then number. As you read the story or text, stop after every few sentences so that you or the student can quickly draw or write something to remind him of what was just read. Although this is time consuming, it helps the student to better understand the topic and to memorize the details.

Assistive reading software allows students to simultaneously hear and see the written word; some software also provides note-taking and highlighting aids, which may be helpful accommodations especially for students who are distracted during reading.

USE OF LANGUAGE

Once students are able to express themselves fluently using novel sentences and are able to request information and respond to basic questions, they are ready to be taught how to speak about past and future events, and how to describe events in ways that a listener is able to understand the sequence. Initially, basic drill of the correct verb tense to describe what happened yesterday, what is happening now, and what will happen tomorrow instills the verb forms that need to be used. Other strategies include:

- Teach correct verb tense using simple worksheets like the one in Figure 5.14.

Figure 5.14   Past, Present, and Future Verb Tenses

Yesterday	Every Day	Right Now	Tomorrow
He _____ fish.	He **eats** fish.	He **is eating** fish.	He _____ fish.
He _____ his milk.	He **drinks** his milk.	He **is drinking** his milk.	He _____ his milk
He _____ out.	He **looks** out.	He **is looking** out.	He _____ out.
He _____ in.	He **walks** in.	He **is walking** in.	He _____ in.
He _____ .	He **coughs**.	He **is coughing**.	He _____ .

- Teach students how to describe a sequence of events using cue cards for "First," "Next," "Then," and "Last," or "Finally."
- Teach students how to describe people, animals, places, objects, events, or feelings. Students must learn what information is salient and of interest to the listener. Figure 5.15 is a sample of a worksheet that can help your student practice this skill.
- Teach students to reciprocate information and ask questions about someone else's information, as in this example:

Peer: "I like swimming."

Your student: "Me, too, I like the pool."

Figure 5.15   Worksheet for Practicing to Describe People, Animals, Places, Objects, Events, or Feelings

Object You Are Describing	It Is _____. (Color)	It Is _____. (Shape)	We ___ With It. (Function)	One More Descriptor
The pumpkin	The pumpkin is orange.	It is round.	We make a jack-o-lantern with it.	Pumpkins are big.
Person You Are Describing	He or She Is a _____. (Occupation)	He or She _____. (What He/She Does)	He or She Works at _____. (Place)	He or She Is _____. (How He/She Feels)
Miss Joy	Miss Joy is a nurse.	She helps sick babies.	She works in the hospital.	She likes her job.

> **Peer:**   "I went to the mall."
>
> **Your student:**   "What did you buy?"

- Teach students to maintain someone else's topic of conversation for an increasing number of turns.
- Teach students to respond to and reciprocate compliments.

Further, very helpful suggestions can be found in the *Teach Me Language: A Language Manual for Children With Autism, Asperger's Syndrome, and Related Developmental Disorders* and companion exercise forms by Sabrina Freeman and Loralei Dake (1997a, 1997b).

PRAGMATICS

Along with having something to say, the student must also learn the rules that govern a conversation, such as body posture, eye gaze, and the signal that indicates when a person is no longer interested in a conversation and wishes to end it or change the topic. Here are some guidelines for teaching such skills:

- Teach your students the appropriate distance to keep between themselves and their communicative partner by giving them specific instructions, preferably in writing, such as, "Stand at least at an arm's length from the person you are speaking with, except when you are standing in line." Simply saying, "Don't stand too close" does not give sufficient information to change a behavior.
- Write instructions in the form of rules on an index card. Rules work like magic for our students! Laminate the card and tape it to the student's desk or hang it on a ring. Here, for instance, is a list of the rules for conversation:

Rules for Conversation

1. Stop.
2. Turn towards the person you are talking to.
3. Look at the person.
4. Say their name, if they are not looking at you.
5. Talk or listen to what they are saying and then answer.

Figure 5.16 An Example of a 5-Point Scale for Loudness

5	TOO LOUD, STOP!
4	Outside voice
3	Great indoor voice
2	A quiet voice
1	Too quiet

- Teach your verbose students with AS to limit the number of sentences on one subject to three or five unless the listener indicates an interest.
- Teach your students to read the body cues of their listener and to modify their conversation accordingly.
- Teach your students to vary their pitch and intonation and to regulate the volume of their speech using visuals such as the 5-Point Scale (Buron & Curtis, 2003) illustrated in Figure 5.16.

The Nonverbal Student

According to the National Research Council (NRC) (2001), it is estimated that between one-third to one-half of individuals with autism do not develop functional speech. Here are several strategies to facilitate communication for this population.

SIGNING

There are advantages to the use of signing because no extra equipment or supplies are needed. However, this strategy is not well suited for students with autism who have fine motor difficulties because they are rarely able to combine more than a few signs together. On the other hand, if they are able to learn a few signs such as "potty," "go," "help," "please," and "eat," these are certainly an important communication support.

THE PICTURE EXCHANGE COMMUNICATION SYSTEM (PECS)

PECS, described earlier in this chapter, is a type of AAC. This strategy, developed specifically for students with autism, emphasizes teaching spontaneous initiation. It is superior to other picture systems and communication boards because it does not require students to have any prerequisite skills.

VOICE OUTPUT COMMUNICATION AIDS (VOCAs)

If a student wishes to engage in the back and forth of conversation—greeting, answering, and asking social questions—they may be ready for other types of AAC, such as VOCAs (Mirenda, 2003). When using a VOCA, the student activates the device by pushing on a picture, or typing, and then the label or phrase is spoken. VOCA systems range from the relatively inexpensive Big Mac, which will utter one word or a short phrase when pushed, to devices costing thousands of dollars with which students can select from many available pictures to form sentences, or type the words, which are then spoken for them. The student who can learn to type may benefit from software such as Write:Out:Loud, which speaks what has been written. This software can be purchased at http://www.donjohnston.com/products/solo/index.html.

If your student is nonverbal, you will want to consult with someone familiar with current AAC systems, such as an assistive technology advisor, the local library, or the special education department at the state level. Whichever system is put in place for your student, here are some steps you can take to ensure ongoing success:

- Allow the student extra time to communicate.
- Create opportunities for the student to communicate.
- Help peers initiate and respond to the student.
- Make sure all assistive devices are in working condition each day by assigning someone to charge batteries when needed and to have the correct overlays ready.
- Quickly update the system with new overlays or pictures when needed.
- Make sure that the student has easy access to his or her communication system throughout the school day.
- Continue to expand the student's ability to use the system.

A question often asked about the use of AAC is whether it will impede verbal language development. There is no evidence that it, in any way, hampers a student's ability or motivation to speak. On the contrary, the communication support offered through signs or pictures may well promote the development of language (Mirenda, 2003).

Social

Wing and Gould (1979) describe autism as a triad of social impairments to emphasize the social nature of the three linked areas of difficulty:

- Impairment of social interaction
- Impairment of social communication
- Impairment of social imagination, flexible thinking, and imaginative play

These social difficulties clearly impact every aspect of a student's life both inside and outside of school. Although teachers are expected to build academic knowledge in their students, there is also the expectation that they will encourage the values and social expectations of our society and culture. While some customs are taught directly (e.g., saying "please" and "thank you"), most are learned through observation of others and by simply having plain common sense. Just as the ability to learn language is innate, so is the social understanding of what is behaviorally and culturally acceptable in our particular society. However, these rules of behavior, often called the "hidden curriculum," are a mystery to many of our students with ASD and must be systematically taught. Once again, it may be helpful to think of the analogy of the students with ASD as people who find themselves in a foreign culture and in need of someone to teach them appropriate behavior. On the other hand, it is also important to remember that appropriate behavior will not always win friendships—especially among children and adolescents. So there is much more to social skills than merely knowing the correct behavior (Myles, Trautman, & Schelvan, 2004).

The ability to interact successfully with others and develop satisfying relationships and friendships is critically linked to the concept of ToM. Simply put, this theory refers to the ability we have to appreciate our own and other people's mental states (beliefs, desires, intentions, knowledge, pretense, and perception) and to understand the links between mental states and action (Baron-Cohen & Swettenham, 1997). Students with ASD typically have delays in this domain and are often described as having mind blindness. This mind blindness makes it difficult for them to understand another person's perspective, as they are often unable to infer how the other is feeling or thinking, and as a result, they are also not able to predict what other people might do (Attwood, 1998). It is no wonder, therefore, that our students with ASD often experience anxiety in social situations—a factor that also needs to be addressed when teaching social skills.

Clearly, our students will need significant social training and support that will include teaching them what to do, how to do it, and then helping them practice doing it. Bellini (2006) suggests following this 5-step model for helping students build social relationships:

1. Assess social functioning: Collect information through interviews, observations, rating scales, and the autism social skills profile (Bellini, 2006).

2. Distinguish between skill acquisition (learning a new skill) and performance deficits (student has the skill, but is not using it).

3. Select intervention strategies to promote skill acquisition and strategies to promote performance.

4. Implement interventions (select peer models, gather resources, find a time and place, and develop a schedule for intervention).

5. Monitor progress using interviews with teachers and parents and rating scales.

As with language, some aspects can be targeted as simple do and don't do rules, but other aspects have to be taught through modeling, understanding and practicing with feedback until they are well embedded in the student's repertoire of skills. Below are a number of interventions that are effective when teaching social skills to our students with ASD.

SOCIAL STORIES

One popular method for teaching social skills is the Social Story (Gray, 1994b). The story, personalized and written in the first person, is particularly helpful to students with ASD as it succinctly presents all the relevant information in a visual and nontransient form. Typically, a Social Story addresses a situation where the student's behavior is unacceptable, such as tantrums because of a change in routine, shouting out in class, hitting instead of asking for help, ignoring peers, hugging strangers, and the like. The story does not give an account of the student's current misbehavior but instead describes the student responding appropriately and the positive consequences that follow. Although originally intended for use with higher-functioning students, Social Stories are also effective with moderately to severely handicapped students (Swaggart et al., 1995).

Social Stories are usually made in printed form with added illustrations—quickly sketched in by the teacher, or more elaborate drawings by the student, or photographs—all showing the student engaging in the appropriate behavior. Social Stories can also be made as PowerPoint or video recorded productions. The decision of what media to use, or whether to use more than one media at a time, will depend on which is most effective for an individual student as well as the teacher's ease in creating and implementing each format (Sansosti & Powell-Smith, 2008). One advantage of the printed form is that it can be read anywhere and anytime it is needed; effective Social Stories can be written quickly and do not need to be elaborate. See below a sample of a Social Story written for a student who frequently cries when engaging with peers. The story should also include pictures of the student and the peers, if possible:

I Can Use My Words

I like to play with my friends in my class. We like to play games together.

Sometimes, one of my friends says or does something that makes me sad or mad.

When that happens, I will say, "Please don't do that" or "I don't like it when you do that."

I can tell my teacher, "Please make him stop." People listen when I use my words.

When I use my words, it makes me feel better.

Here are some guidelines for writing a Social Story (Gray & Garand, 1993):

- Choose one situation that is difficult for the student, and gather information on the specific activity, the location, other people involved, the student's behavior, and, if possible, the student's view of the situation.
- Keep the narrative simple and keep the main point salient; the more details you add the less clear it may become to the student.
- Tailor the story to the student's level of comprehension. For students who are not readers yet, use pictures with few words.
- Use a combination of descriptive, directive, and perspective sentences; for every one directive statement, use at least two to five descriptive and perspective sentences. Descriptive sentences are those that objectively define where a situation occurs, who is involved, what they are doing, and why it is happening (e.g., "At the end of recess, when the teacher blows the whistle, it is time to line up outside the school door"). Directive sentences state the required response of the student in the specific social situation (e.g., "As soon as I hear the whistle, I run to the door to line up"). Make sure your directive sentences are stated positively instead of describing problem behaviors (e.g., do not say, "When the whistle blows, I will not sit down on the ground and pretend not to know it is time to go in"). Perspective sentences describe the reactions and feelings of others (e.g., "My friends and teachers are glad when I get to the line quickly").
- Personalize the story. Use the student's own name and write it in the first person, present tense.
- Avoid words such as always; instead, use words such as usually or sometimes (e.g., "When I see a friend at the mall he usually says, "Hi!"").

Once written, introduce the story to the student in a quiet place with few distractions. Read the story to the student at least once a day, and, if possible, just before the problematic situation; also consider sending a copy home for the parents or student to read when not in school. The story can also serve to inform others so that everyone has the same behavioral expectations for the student; you may even have the student share the story with other team members. Once the desired behavior is demonstrated, continue to keep the story accessible and review it frequently.

POWER CARDS

Another popular tool is the Power Card (Gagnon, 2001), which takes advantage of a student's area of interest to help him follow routines or engage in appropriate behavior. This two-part strategy consists of a script and a Power Card: The script is a short narrative that describes the problem behavior and how the student's special interest or hero addresses this situation, the three to five specific steps that are taken by the special interest or hero, and how the student can do likewise to have the same success as the hero or special interest; the Power Card lists these same three to five steps, along with a picture of the hero or special interest. This card can then be carried around or placed in strategic locations to remind the student how to behave in certain situations. Typically, Power Cards are made on cards the size of a business card, trading card, or bookmark. For example, Paulo, who is passionate about cars, might have a Power Card script that looks like this:

Car Experts Write It All Down

Car experts lead an exciting life! Some make cars, some fix cars, and some race cars. Often, they just want to do the math in their head and not write it down. However, they know it is very important to be able to check their work to be sure it is correct and so that others can see the solutions to the problems. For these reasons, car experts do the following three things:

1. Write down the steps to solve Math problems.
2. Write neatly.
3. Hand over the information to the people who need to see it.

Car experts know that when students do these three things at school, they are practicing the skills they will need when they become a car expert.

The Power Card would then list the three most important points that Paulo must remember along with a picture of a car (Figure 5.17).

Figure 5.17 An Example of a Power Card

A car expert will

- write out all the steps in the math solutions,
- write neatly, and
- hand in his work each day.

Paulo could attach this card to his desk at school or inside his math book; a power card can be placed in the locker, inside a planner or wallet, on the mirror at home, or wherever the student might need to use it.

RULE CARDS

Our students often need to have the appropriate steps involved in a social situation spelled out for them. Because they are concrete thinkers, it is helpful to have this information in written form and stated clearly in the form of rules. Figure 5.18 is a simple example of a set of rules to use when asking peers to play.

Figure 5.18   An Example of a Rule Card

Asking to Play Rules

1. Call the person's name.
2. Look at the person.
3. Smile.
4. Ask, "Can I join you?" or "Can I play with you?"
5. If they say, "Yes," you say, "Great!" If they say "No," you say, "OK," and walk away.

It is especially important to make sure that students are aware of the social conventions (the hidden curriculum) in the areas of bathroom use, sexuality, encounters with law enforcement, and talking to teachers and other adults. Lack of awareness of these unwritten social rules might well cause great embarrassment and even trouble with the authorities (Packer, 1997).

CIRCLE OF FRIENDS

Students with ASD have difficulty making and keeping friends; they need to be taught the how-to of friendship. A simple yet effective method for promoting peer relationships and increasing social skills is to create a Circle of Friends program around the student. The Circle of Friends provides a supportive social and emotional framework at school that promotes peer interaction. Typically a Circle of Friends has the following components:

- It has four to five members including the student with ASD. The teacher chooses the team members based on their ability to be good role models and based on their shared interests.
- It is completely voluntary.
- One adult is in charge of the meetings, organizes them, and oversees them to provide direction and feedback.
- It meets once a week for about 30 minutes during recess, lunch, or after school.
- The purpose of these meetings is to participate in a mutually pleasing activity (e.g., playing Monopoly or eating lunch together).
- The activity provides an opportunity to work on peer relationships and to discuss how to resolve conflict situations that may have occurred during the previous week.

Once you have chosen the students that you would like to invite to participate in this activity, you will have to ask for their parents' permission. See Resource J for an example of such a letter.

THE 5-POINT SCALE

Students with ASD tend to see things as black and white, good or bad, and go from feeling totally calm to being ready to explode without understanding that there is a range of feelings between the extremes. An intervention that helps students realize there are points in between the extremes of feelings and behavior is the 5-Point Scale (Buron & Curtis, 2003). This scale allows students to come to grips with their feelings, as well as their behaviors and others' reactions to their behaviors, by providing a simple and concrete visual display as illustrated in Figure 5.19.

The 5-Point Scale was developed for a 14-year-old boy, Joe, a ninth grader, who had lashed out physically at teachers and peers on several occasions. Joe was doing well in school but had trouble realizing when he was getting overwhelmed by work, social, or environmental demands. He, along with his teacher and parents, made this visual scale to help him assess his feelings. He kept a copy in his planner at school and one at home so he could review it frequently. From time to time during the day, his teachers would ask him what number best described him at that moment to teach him to become more aware of how he was feeling. Joe needed to call home several times, but for the most part, he was able to ask for help from the staff when he reached a 3, and his physical aggression was totally eliminated. Scales such as the one above should be custom made for the student and when possible have the student help you write it.

Figure 5.19 A Sample of a 5-Point Scale

5	Out of control	I never let this happen!	Out of control means the police might get involved.
4	Very tense	I have left the situation and called home.	My parents understand and they listen to me carefully. They will help me quickly.
3	Tense	I have told a teacher or paraeducator, "I need a break now."	Others are glad I am asking for help—they will help me quickly.
2	A little uneasy	I can handle this feeling by myself, but I make sure I know how to get help if I need it.	Others still don't need to help me with my feelings.
1	Feeling calm	I can participate in activities without help.	Others don't need to help me with my feelings.

ROLE-PLAYING

Role-playing involves having students practice a social skill with you or with peers in a quiet and private place where they can feel at ease. You may prime the student with some verbal or written directives beforehand and then provide a script or model for them to follow as they role play. Initially, you and the peers may need to also prompt the student. For this to be an effective learning experience for your student, keep the atmosphere relaxed and enjoyable for all involved (Bellini, 2006). This approach has the advantage of being much more likely to generalize to the real-world setting than when the student is just told what to do.

In addition, roles can be reversed, which helps students gain the other person's perspective and allows you an opportunity to discuss the different feelings involved in the roles.

VIDEO MODELING

A more time-consuming, yet powerful technique is video modeling and video self-modeling (Charlop & Milstein, 1989; Sigafoos, O'Reilly, & de la Cruz, 2007). In video modeling students watch others perform the target behavior while in video self-modeling students observe themselves engaging in the desired behavior. Both forms of video modeling allow students to view and review the different elements of appropriate behavior. Although videotaping students with ASD engaging in the appropriate behavior will require more time and effort, it may be more reinforcing and therefore worth the extra effort. When students perform the target skill, such as raising their hand in class when asked a question, record this segment and show it over and over again. If you are targeting a sequence of skills, such as initiating and maintaining a conversation, you may need to videotape several occasions and splice them together to provide a complete model for the student (Bellini, 2006). This technique involves some knowledge of video editing, but it is a highly effective approach to teaching social skills.

SOCIAL AUTOPSIES AND CARTOONING

Social autopsies, combined with cartooning, are very helpful for students with AS. By social autopsies, we refer to conducting a review of a social situation with the student to help him or her understand why it did not work out well; by cartooning, we refer to drawing out a situation using simple stick figures and adding speech and thought bubbles thus making the scene more concrete for the student. Here is a real-life example that demonstrates a typical social misunderstanding:

Chad is a highly verbal third grader with AS who is learning how to make and keep friends. One morning he walks up to his best friend Marta and immediately says, "I hate your T-shirt." Marta is first surprised but then quickly responds with, "Well, I hate you, too!" and walks away. Chad in turn grabs Marta and pushes her to the ground. Of course there are hurt feelings all round, and now Chad is in trouble and sent to the principal.

As soon as possible, the teacher helps Chad and Maria understand what went wrong by drawing out the scenario using stick figures. What they said and thought are put into speech and thought bubbles. Chad's comment, "I hate your T-shirt," was put into his speech bubble; what he was thinking, "I need to tell my friend that I don't like her T-shirt so that the other kids won't make fun of her," was placed in his thought bubble. What Maria thought, "Chad hates me! I am sad," was put in her thought bubble, and what she said, "Well, I hate you, too!" was put in the speech bubble. In this way, cartooning allows both students to understand how the other felt and why he or she acted that way. The final step in the process is to rehearse how the student could have tackled the situation more appropriately (Gray, 1994a).

PLAY

This section on sociocommunicative interventions would not be complete without a word about play. One of the distinguishing marks of young students with autism is that they lack imaginative play, and indeed, many students with autism do not engage in any form of play during unstructured time. On the playground it is not uncommon to observe them alone, entertaining themselves by running around, or by engaging in stereotypic behaviors of one sort or another. Thus, while the typical peers are engaged socially during recess, the students with ASD seem odd and out of place. While playing, students also learn what activities to do during leisure time. Play skills are, thus, important life skills for all individuals to acquire, including those with ASD, and these skills need to be targeted in the students' educational plan at an early age (National Research Council, 2001).

An educational plan that promotes play skills should focus on teaching students how to interact with play materials appropriately, as well as how to play with peers. Some of the play skills to teach include imitating actions of peers, following directions from peers, reciprocating and initiating greetings, answering and reciprocating social questions, responding to peer play-initiation statements, requesting peers to play, and engaging in play with peers. Here are some specific interventions that promote play skill acquisition:

- On the playground, students with ASD tend to play on the same equipment over and over again. Gradually, teach your student to add new equipment to his play repertoire, using a visual schedule along with shaping and reinforcement techniques.
- Engineer social interactions with typical peers for a certain amount of time by structuring activities that require turn taking, looking at and communicating with a play partner. Such games may include throwing a ball to each other, playing a board game, or sharing a computer game. You may start implementing social interaction activities with one peer, gradually increasing the complexity of the social interactions by adding more peers.
- Provide a script to support communication. Rather than telling the student, "Say _____," provide a cue card with the words that are needed. Remember that a visual cue is easier to fade than a verbal prompt.
- Coach the play partner on how to respond to communication attempts made by the student with ASD.
- Coach the student with ASD on what to do or say to continue the play interaction with peers.
- During center time, students with ASD may tend to avoid playing with certain materials, such as sand in the sandbox or paint during an art project. When this occurs, desensitize students by physically prompting them to touch the aversive material for short periods of time and gradually increasing expectations. When students become comfortable with the new materials, start engineering social interactions with peers, such as pouring contents from a container held by the peer into the one held by the student with ASD or passing out materials to each other.
- Teach peer imitation. Seat the student with ASD and a peer at a table facing each other. Ask the peer to perform the behaviors shown in a photograph (e.g., a person clapping hands), and teach the student with ASD to imitate his peer. Once mastered in this highly controlled environment, move to teaching peer imitation through the game follow the leader. Ask a peer to perform a series of activities (e.g., jumping, climbing, or throwing a ball into a bucket) and teach the student with ASD to follow.
- Teach the student to engage in specific play and leisure activities using independent activity schedules (McClannahan & Krantz, 1999). This is one of our favorite interventions for helping students who have not yet learned how to play with any toys or materials appropriately.
- Keep play time lighthearted so that it can serve as a release valve for the prevailing anxiety amongst our students with ASD.
- Videotape play times and edit the tape so that the student can watch himself or herself being successful. Watching him- or herself being successful again and again builds up the student's sense of competence and pleasure.

As students get older, they may well develop a passion for video games shared also by peers, which can provide for a conversation topic. However, team sports, which bring other students together, will probably not be a favorite activity, but if it is, celebrate it! Students with ASD often prefer activities in which they can compete against themselves and not others, such as swimming and track. Weight lifting is another beneficial lifelong learning activity that can provide pleasure, health benefits, and companionship alongside others who engage in the same activity.

RECESS, LUNCHROOM, AND PHYSICAL EDUCATION

During the most unstructured times of the day, such as recess, lunchtime, and even during PE, our students with ASD often need adult support and instruction.

Recess

For instance, during recess, they may just wander around the perimeter of the playground, not knowing how to enter into play with others or they enter awkwardly and are then rebuffed. Because our students are rule driven, it is especially hard for them to adjust to the rather fluid rules of recess interactions. Simply telling our students what to do is usually not sufficient; instead, along with staff support, you will want to use some of the strategies described above such as Circle of Friends, Social Stories, Power Cards, written rules, modeling, or video modeling. Recess provides a unique opportunity for teachers to systematically work on basic social, play, and communication skills—so choose your goals and engineer the environment if necessary so that you can work on them. Here are some basic guidelines to remember:

- Start with simple games that require some turn taking and simple scripted language exchange, if necessary.
- Involve high-status peers.
- Choose activities of interest to the student and his or her peers.
- Start with one peer and gradually increase the number of participants and the sophistication of the games.
- When working with a young student who will not even try out the different playground equipment, use a visual schedule to direct the student to a variety of areas on the playground.

Lunchroom

Lunchtime also reveals a student's deficits in social and communication skills and, particularly, the lack of understanding of the hidden curriculum; sensory issues, such as the noise level and the smells, may cause discomfort. Therefore, provide sufficient support during lunchtime to ensure the student's success—do not wait until the student is causing trouble!

Physical Education (PE)

For many students, PE can be uniquely challenging. Not only is it a less structured time, the noise, activity level, and possibly the smells of the gymnasium can all cause sensory overload; the social expectations for adolescents in a locker room may be a complete mystery to our students with ASD; and either the need to win at all cost or the lack of coordination are factors that make team sports very challenging. For these reasons, it is vital to make sure that our students have supervision and support during PE to look out for their welfare and to teach them social and physical skills for them to enjoy this time with peers. Once in secondary school, it may be helpful to put PE at the end of the day so that any stress that builds up during that hour does not transfer to other classes. It is sometimes necessary to excuse students from taking PE at school and allowing them to earn the credit through preapproved outside activities, such as documented participation at a local gym.

BULLYING

We are all aware that bullying is a serious issue among students in general; still those with ASD tend to become victims of bullying, harassment, and teasing far more often. These students are more likely to become targets of such acts because they tend to stand out, to be loners, and are often perceived as different and strange by their peers. They frequently misunderstand social situations causing them to react inappropriately, and because of social and communication deficits, their coping skills are poor. It is no wonder then that many have heightened anxiety and even depression, seriously affecting their well-being. Every effort must be made by school staff to protect our students from bullying and here are some ideas:

- Provide direct and explicit instruction on communication, social skills, and problem solving.
- Provide supervision, especially during unstructured situations such as lunch, recess, halls, and locker rooms.
- Educate peers on how to prevent bullying.
- Recruit high-status peers to interact with the student with ASD.
- Have a school- and a classroom-wide policy of zero tolerance for bullying.
- Take all reports of bullying seriously.

Applied Behavior Analysis (ABA)

ABA is a set of principles that has proved to be highly effective in teaching students in general, and those with ASD in particular. When using an ABA framework, you first select a behavior to teach, and then systematically teach it by taking small manageable steps toward the goal while reinforcing correct responses. ABA includes the principles of reinforcement, DTT, task analysis, prompting and prompt fading, shaping, and errorless learning strategies. We will discuss each of these principles, including data collection systems and how they may be used with any student on the spectrum.

Reinforcement

When teaching a new set of skills or behaviors, whether it is working through a math page quickly or not shouting out in class, reinforcement principles will be strategic to your success. Reinforcement means any consequence that follows a behavior that makes it more likely to occur again in the future. Reinforcement can be either positive or negative. Positive reinforcement occurs when the consequence of a behavior is pleasing to the student and when it increases the probability of the behavior reoccurring. For example, if we know that Idan loves to read books, we may tell him that he may read his book when his work is finished.

Remember: Reinforcers work best when you present them visually (see the First . . . Then card on p. 48) and when you present the student with a menu of reinforcers to choose from.

Negative reinforcement refers to a consequence that is aversive or unpleasant to the student but still one that increases the probability that the behavior it follows will reoccur in the future. If we know, for example, that Noah loves recess, we may tell him that any work that does not get done will have to be completed during recess. So if Noah does not want to miss out on recess, he will probably choose to work diligently on his paper. In other words, the fear of losing the recess (an unpleasant consequence) will increase the probability that Noah will complete his work.

Types of Reinforcers

Generally, there are two kinds of reinforcers—primary reinforcers and secondary reinforcers (Alberto & Troutman, 2008). Primary reinforcers are concrete and are intended to give physical comfort or pleasure; they include edibles and sensory input. Secondary reinforcers are symbolic, and they include tangible reinforcers such as stickers or intangible reinforcers such as teacher's praise. Table 5.2 summarizes the types of reinforcers.

Remember: The younger and the lower functioning a student is the more we rely on primary reinforcers.

IDENTIFYING REINFORCERS FOR YOUR STUDENTS

Finding what motivates your students is crucial to your ability to teach them. With some students, for example middle school students with AS, simply giving them a list of possible reinforcers to choose from works well (e.g., "Do you

Table 5.2   Types of Reinforcers

Group	Types	Open- and Closed-Ended	Examples
Primary reinforcers	1. Edibles	Closed	Foods and drinks
	2. Toys	Open Closed	Blocks Puzzle
	3. Sensory input (auditory, visual, tactile, olfactory, or kinesthetic)	Mostly open	Music, swing, blanket, Koosh ball, tickling, and toys that provide visual input
Secondary reinforcers	1. Tangible reinforcers	Closed	Pennies, tokens, stickers, points, and grades
	2. Intangible reinforcers	Closed	Smiles, hugs, words of praise, and voice modulation that expresses excitement

want to work for 5 minutes on the computer, for a granola bar, for 10 minutes in the library, or is there something else you would like to work for?"). However, with young students or with those who are developmentally delayed, the teacher will need to be the one to identify the reinforcers. Here are some ideas to help you identify your student's incentives:

- Observe students during free play to see what items they choose. Young students may choose to play with items that provide auditory or visual input, some may choose to engage in repetitive activities such as lining up cars, and teenagers may choose to play video games.
- Ask the student's caregivers what are the student's preferred activities and preferred items to drink or eat.
- Conduct a systematic assessment of your student's preferred reinforcements. During the assessment process, show your student no more than five items at a time from various categories, such as food items, sensory objects, and toys. Keep a tally of what your student reaches for until you have identified the three top choices.

Remember: Students are sometimes reinforced by very peculiar items, such as shiny objects, and mundane activities, such as a walk around the school, a visit to the school library, or sitting by a favorite person.

Use of Reinforcers

It is helpful to identify reinforcers that are both open ended and closed ended. Closed-ended reinforcers include food items or toys that have a natural ending, such as a puzzle or a shape sorter. An open-ended reinforcer, on the other hand, has no natural ending; a student can play with it for as long as he or she wishes, such as drawing a picture or playing a video game.

Reinforcers that are closed ended, such as eating an M&M, are sometimes easier to use because once the piece of candy has been eaten, the student can immediately begin to earn another one. An open-ended activity, however, such as playing with blocks or watching a portion of a movie, is more time consuming and it requires more effort to redirect the student back to work. When doing an open-ended activity, use a timer to signal to the student that the reinforcement is over.

Do not forget to pair a social reinforcer with a tangible reinforcer to teach students to respond to praise and attention. When praising, try varying the expressions you use with words such as "good," "good job," "yeah," "great," "super," "way to go," "right," and "fantastic," while identifying the action praised whenever possible: "Nice waiting, John!" More importantly, it is the positive tone of voice and facial expression that signals success to the student. Often, it is a good use of your time to simply repeat the correct answer the student has given; for example, "Yes, John! Plants need water and sunshine to grow." This both reinforces and cements the knowledge being learned.

When you first begin to teach a new skill, use a 1:1 rate of reinforcement (one reinforcer for each response). As the student masters a skill start decreasing the rate of reinforcement (i.e., reinforce only every third or fifth response). For behaviors that need only maintenance reinforce only every several correct responses. This technique is based on the same principle of human behavior that keeps gamblers playing slot machines for hours; even though a slot machine does not give a return for each game, the occasional monetary return provides a gambler with the incentive to keep inserting money. Such a schedule teaches a student to delay gratification, and it is powerful in maintaining desired behaviors, so we recommend that you move to such a schedule as soon as possible. This means that a student should be expected to gradually show an increasingly higher rate of desired behaviors before he or she is allowed access to a reinforcer. In this way, students will gradually learn to respond more readily to the teacher's instructions and to the natural consequences in the environment.

If your student stops making progress and is even starting to regress, consider the following questions:

- Do you need different reinforcers? Examine what needs to be changed in regard to the selection of reinforcers or the reinforcement schedule. It is important to remember that items that have been strong reinforcers in the past may lose their effectiveness and new reinforcers will need to be found.
- Do you need a different rate of reinforcement? You may need to increase the reinforcement rate from time to time if you lose the student's attention or if behavior becomes difficult. In such a case, start making easy demands that you know the student can readily comply with to ensure that he or she can earn the reinforcer. Once the student is back on track, you are now ready to return to the task that you had been working on.

As soon as possible, though, you will want to transfer your student to secondary reinforcers, which are more socially acceptable in the general classroom. Token systems are one of the ways this can be accomplished.

TOKEN SYSTEMS

Token systems are a way to reinforce desired behaviors with a concrete token that can later be exchanged for a variety of desired events or items the student wants. It is an extremely useful way of visually displaying for the student that his or her behavior is earning him or her a desired reinforcer. Simply saying to a student with autism, "Do all your work and behave properly so that you can play with the race car set," is unlikely to change the student's behavior. On the other hand, saying to the student, "I will give you a token each time you finish writing a sentence; when you have 10 tokens you can play with the race car set for 10 minutes," is much more likely to produce a change in behavior.

The tokens can be poker chips, pennies, checkmarks, tickets, happy faces, points, or anything that can be added up and then exchanged for something the student wants. When using a token system, first have the student choose a reinforcer from a list or picture display. Then let the student know specifically how many tokens will be needed to exchange for the reinforcer and exactly what specific behavior(s) will be reinforced. As discussed above, you may deliver the tokens after each correct response or after a series of correct responses, depending on the task's difficulty. It is important to keep the system simple so that it is not a time waster nor too complicated to remember. The student must clearly see the tokens accumulate as they are earned and should then have access to the reinforcer as soon as he or she has accumulated the needed number of tokens.

Once the desired behaviors are well established, the token system can be gradually faded. This is accomplished by continuously thinning out the delivery of tokens and by consistently pairing the tokens with social praise so that in time the social praise will be sufficient to maintain the desired behavior.

TOKEN BOARDS

A token board is simply another way of making the delivery of tokens concrete and manageable for both the teacher and the student. They can be made of laminated construction paper or clip boards. On one side of the board, at the top, put a long strip of Velcro, long enough to hold 10 small tokens (pennies). Below the strip put 10 individual small pieces of Velcro in a semicircle. Underneath this semicircle, in the middle, put another piece of Velcro (see Figure 5.20). The other side of the board should have several lines of Velcro to hold icons of the reinforcers (see Figure 5.21). Alternatively, you may choose to use a three-ring binder to hold the student's reinforcers, as described in the Where to Store the Reinforcer Icons section.

Figure 5.20 A Token Board

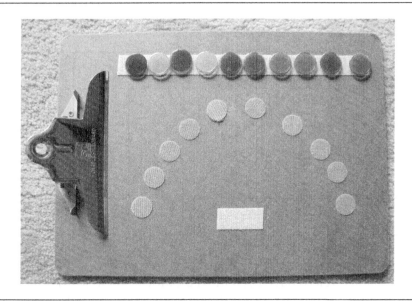

Figure 5.21 Backside of a Token Board

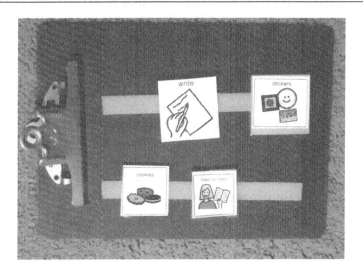

Make sure you start by presenting your student with his or her menu of reinforcers and by asking, "What do you want to work for?" Place the icon representing his or her choice on the board on top of the piece of Velcro underneath the semicircle. You will have already decided how many tokens you want your student to earn in exchange for a reinforcer, and you have already placed that number of tokens on the top long strip of Velcro. Every time the student responds correctly, reinforce the response by moving one token from

Figure 5.22 A Reinforcement Chart

I am working for _____.

the top long strip to an individual piece in the semicircle. When all tokens from the top long Velcro have been moved to the semicircle, the student earns the reinforcer. When a task becomes easy for your student, expect correct responses to several instructions before reinforcing with a token.

See Figure 5.22 for another example of a token system. Once students choose what to work for, you may tell them that they can earn it when all the 5 or 10 squares in a row are marked (with a checkmark, a sticker, or a stamp). Some teachers laminate the reinforcement grid and use a dry erase marker, while others like to simply use a fresh grid and send completed ones home. On a tough day, you will reinforce more liberally by giving checkmarks quickly for appropriate behavior, or you will reduce the number of check-marks needed to earn the chosen reinforcer. This type of visual reinforcement system may be easier to use in a general education classroom as it is less con-spicuous and, therefore, more socially acceptable. You may find a blank rein-forcement chart that you can duplicate in Resource K.

Where to Store the Reinforcer Icons

Icons of reinforcers can be housed either on the back side of a token board or in a three-ring binder. If a student's reinforcers menu is limited to a few pre-ferred items, housing the icons on the back side of a token board can work well. However, for a student whose repertoire of choices is considerable, or for a student who is nonverbal, using a three-ring-binder can work more effec-tively. In this case, to make scanning for an item quick and easy, color code the pages based on topic. For example, for Karli, we placed all the icons for food items on a yellow page, all the icons for color adjectives on a green page, all the icons for toys on a blue page, and all the icons for activities on a brown page. So if Karli wanted a red Skittle, she would go to the yellow page to pick up the Skittle icon, and then she would go to the green page to pick out the red color because the red Skittle was her favorite.

Discrete Trial Teaching (DTT)

Students with autism often learn best when required to focus in on the different aspects of a new skill and when given multiple opportunities for practicing them. DTT is uniquely suited for teaching students with autism as it takes these characteristics into account. DTT refers to the teaching of a skill by breaking it down into small, distinctive steps. Each step is taught through a series of trials (Earles-Vollrath, Cook, Robbins, & Ben-Arieh, 2008). Each trial consists of three parts: (1) teacher's instruction (e.g., "Who flies a plane?"); (2) student's response; and (3) consequence for a response, that is, reinforcement based on the correctness of the response (Anderson, Taras, & Cannon, 1996; Maurice, Green, & Luce, 1996). Figure 5.23 illustrates an example of a discrete trial.

When using the DTT method as described above, start by setting up the environment for success:

- Find a small, private space outside the classroom, or if you must stay in the classroom, ensure that the work area is quiet and free from distractions by using furniture or dividers to create a small area separated off from the rest of the classroom.
- Remove nonessential items from the table.
- Check that the student's chair is the correct height and feet reach the floor comfortably.
- Be well prepared before the beginning of each instruction session. You must know what you are going to teach, how you are going to break it down into manageable steps, as well as how you are going to reinforce.
- Have all the materials and reinforcers at hand including data collection forms ready to use. If you expect students to sit and wait while you organize your materials, chances are that they will start to engage in inappropriate behaviors and precious time will be wasted as you attempt to get them resettled for work. Once students are seated, proceed with teaching as follows:
  - Present the reinforcement menu (i.e., the visual icons of reinforcers) and ask, "What would you like to work for?"

Figure 5.23 Components of Discrete Trial Instruction

Teacher's Instruction	Student's Response	Consequence
"What is it?"	"A pen."	"Yes! It's a pen!"
Instructor holds up a pen.		Instructor provides consequence (reinforcement), praise, and a tangible item (e.g., an edible or a game).

o Place the icon on the token board to remind the student throughout the session what he or she is working for.

o Gain the student's attention and begin instruction.

o Initially keep instructions short and simple, avoid extra words that do not add to the meaning (e.g., "please"). Later you may vary your instructions to help him or her generalize the skill. Allow the student only a few seconds to respond.

o If the student fails to respond correctly, provide a prompt to assist him or her in a correct response. It is important to know precisely what your criterion is for correct responding and to make sure that everyone working with the student maintains the same criteria.

PACE AND INTERSPERSING MAINTENANCE AND NEW TASKS

- Keep the pace of the lesson brisk; if you present your instructions too slowly or too fast, you may lose your student's interest.
- Intersperse easy already mastered tasks amongst the new ones. The recommended ratio of easy tasks to difficult ones is 80% to 20%. Interspersing various types of instructions also ensures that the student pays attention to your instruction and does not repeat a response automatically.

DATA COLLECTION

Plan to start each session by probing the skills in the program (see a data collection form in Resource E). In DTT probing is a form of pretesting skills immediately before teaching them on a daily basis; it is a way to check whether a specific skill in a program has been mastered. Suppose that your program involves teaching your student to follow 5 one-step instructions. Your probe sheet will have those five instructions listed twice. After your student has made his or her choice of a reinforcer, start by asking him or her to perform the first skill listed on your probe sheet and mark whether the response was correct or incorrect without giving the student any feedback. Follow this by a request to perform a skill that is easy for him or her. Once the student performs this task— the one that you are not probing—reinforce him or her. Because this is a test, we do not want to give any feedback regarding the items that we are in the process of teaching. However, because we still need to keep the student excited and interested in working, we are going to reinforce those skills that he or she has already mastered.

Once the probing is complete, use the information gathered as a guide for this teaching session. During this teaching session, you do not need to collect any further data on the skill you are teaching.

Task Analysis

Task analysis is a useful concept that will help you in teaching all students with disabilities, especially those with ASD. Task analysis is breaking down a skill into small steps that are then taught in order, either in the form of a forward chain, starting with the first step in the procedure, or a backward chain, starting with the last step in a procedure. When teaching a student to take his or her socks off, for example, the first step in a forward-chaining procedure might be inserting both her thumbs inside the sock. Backward chaining has been found useful in the teaching of daily living routines, such as washing hands. In this case, the first step to teach would be drying hands. You may find that a student with ASD is not able to independently complete the steps involved in the beginning of the day routine, which may include hanging up coat, putting away backpack, sitting down, getting out books and homework, getting a pencil, and morning seat work, and completing the independent work. In conducting a task analysis, it is important to take data on where the student experiences a breakdown in the routine or chain of events. Here are some important issues to remember when conducting a task analysis:

- The task analysis should contain all necessary steps for the student to complete the task.
- The steps in the task analysis should be listed in a logical sequence.
- Choosing whether to use a forward- or a backward-chaining procedure depends on the type of task, prerequisite skills, and probability to succeed.

Prompting and Prompt Fading

Prompting is the act of providing a student the necessary assistance to complete a task. There are various levels of prompts ranging from least to most intrusive (see Table 5.3). When a student does not respond to environmental cues, such as going to the carpet for group time after breakfast or going to lunch hall when the bell rings, start with the lowest level of prompt—verbal instruction. If the student fails to respond in about five seconds, move on to the next prompt level; that is, repeat the verbal instruction and this time add a gesture, such as pointing, and so on.

Once you have determined the student's ability to perform a certain task, start teaching it by providing the level of prompt that ensures his or her success. When the student starts performing the task consistently, it is time to provide a lower-level prompt. Prompt fading is the process of gradually reducing teacher prompts until the student can perform a task independently.

It is important to keep in mind, though, that there is a procedural difference between teaching random new skills and teaching routines, such as hand washing. When explaining to a student with AS the meaning of a specific figure of speech, for example, a teacher will use examples and verbal clarifications. However, to teach a student the process of hand washing, use

Table 5.3   Prompt Levels

Levels	Description
First	Environmental cues
Second	Verbal instruction
Third	Verbal instruction plus gesture
Fourth	Verbal instruction plus partial physical guidance
Fifth	Total physical guidance
Sixth	Verbal instruction plus total physical guidance

only physical guidance from behind rather than talking through the steps. By using this method, you will avoid building yourself in as an additional step in the process of carrying out the task. So when teaching a chain of actions in a routine, put the student through the actions using full or partial physical prompt with no verbal cueing; that is, teach by doing rather than by telling. As he or she becomes successful, start to gradually fade the physical prompt.

Another useful prompting procedure is known as delayed prompting. Delayed prompting is an effective procedure to use when teaching a new skill. When teaching a student, for example, to reply to the question, "What is your name?" you will start by providing him or her with the answer immediately (full prompt). At this stage, the student will be reinforced for simply repeating the answer. As the student becomes successful, start to pause between the question and the reply, to allow him or her to start responding before the prompt is provided (beat the prompt). Gradually, increase the pause time to allow the student to respond to the question independently.

Shaping

Shaping occurs when you reinforce approximations of a behavior until the student performs it independently. When teaching a new skill, start by reinforcing every attempt the student makes towards a target behavior, even when these attempts are prompted. Then gradually expect the student to improve his or her performance before you reinforce, until he or she masters the skill. Say, for example, that you want to increase on-task behavior for your student during journal writing. In this case, you might start by reinforcing on-task behavior for a very short length of time, perhaps after he or she writes one sentence. Starting with an easy expectation has two purposes: (1) to start building success and (2) to teach the student the system—"The sooner I complete the undesirable task, the faster I get access to my reinforcer." As the completion of the task becomes easy and the student is successful, expect him or her to write two sentences to gain access to a reinforcer and so on. The idea is to be sure to reinforce incremental improvements.

Errorless Learning Strategies

Errorless learning strategies refer to strategies that maximize a student's likelihood to provide a correct response. When teaching a new skill, we provide as many cues and as much prompting as needed to ensure that the student gives a correct response. For instance, when teaching a student to receptively discriminate between the picture of an apple and that of other photographs, we will start by placing the picture of an apple closest to the student and in the most salient position on the table. The photograph of another item (the distractor) will be placed at an inconspicuous place on the table. We will instruct the student to point to the apple, while making sure that we redirect his or her point if he or she begins to point to the wrong card, thus preventing the student from making a mistake. This approach continues even as other cards are brought closer to the target card.

Data Collection

Data collection is an important component of ABA. As an educator, you are well aware of the importance of tests to guide your teaching as well as being thoroughly familiar with all the types of tests typically used in a class, such as summative and formative tests. This section is not meant to discuss data collection involved in typical classroom situations. Rather, we are discussing data collection in the context of ABA and when working with students with autism, who require individualized interventions such as those targeted to increase students' social skills or decrease maladaptive behaviors. There are several ways to collect such data. We will describe below the three most common ones in the classroom setting: event/frequency, time sampling, and duration. Which of these you choose is obviously determined by the behavior or skill that you are measuring. These methods for collecting data are not all inclusive, and for a more in-depth discussion of all the possible ways to record data, please consult *Applied Behavior Analysis for Teachers* (Alberto & Troutman, 2008).

EVENT (FREQUENCY) RECORDING

Use event (frequency) recording to collect data on the number of times a behavior occurs. If, for example, you are interested in decreasing the number of inappropriate comments made by a student during one class period, you may decide to use frequency recording, that is, marking every time an inappropriate comment is made. See a sample of such a form in Resource E. If the frequency of inappropriate comments is high, you may decide to use an average of three-day data points as your baseline. If, however, the frequency is low, you will probably decide to calculate the data on a weekly basis and use a week average as your baseline.

TIME SAMPLING

Time sampling is helpful to use when the behavior you are monitoring occurs at a high rate or over an extended period of time, such as off-task behavior. To take time sampling data, you may use a form that has a series of boxes representing intervals of time. So, for example, if you wish to know for how long Matt stays off-task during a period of 20 minutes in math, you may choose to divide this period into 2-minute intervals (see Figure 5.10). At the end of every 2 minutes, the teacher needs to look at Matt to see whether he is on task and record this in the data collection form.

This recording is somewhat challenging for you as a classroom teacher because it necessitates the use of a timer or a tape recorder with timed beeps for the chosen intervals to remind you to check the presence or absence of the behavior and to move on to the next time segment. The data in Figure 5.10 means that during a 20-minute work period Matt is off task 12 minutes (60%). You may want to take such data over the next three to four days to get an average score that will constitute your baseline. A time sampling recording form can be found in Resource E.

DURATION

Duration is a useful way to collect data when a teacher is concerned about the length of time a behavior occurs. For example, Diana takes a long time to wash her hands, which interferes with her ability to participate in all classroom activities. So you decide to decrease the time Diana spends washing her hands. To measure the length of time that it takes Diana to wash her hands, you will use duration data. For this type of data collection, you will need a stopwatch. After collecting this data on three consecutive instances of hand washing, you can calculate an average of the length of time that it takes Diana to wash her hands, which will serve as your baseline.

Here are few items to consider when collecting data on a behavior:

- Decide the frequency of data collection during the intervention period. Of course, this also depends on the type of behavior or skill that you are monitoring. Keep in mind, though, that data collection should not become so burdensome that it interferes with teaching. Often, collecting data for limited periods of time and only a few times a week will provide the necessary information.

- Decide the location of data collection. The data collected during the intervention period needs to relate to the data obtained to establish the baseline. That is, if the baseline was established during a math class, the data during the intervention period should also be taken during math.
- Get all materials ready for the data collection.
- Decide the actual technique to use to collect the data in the classroom. Here are several ideas:
    o Have the data collection form and writing instrument attached to a clipboard that you either carry around if you need to use it in different environments or keep it in a certain location that you can access easily.
    o Have an index card attached to a lanyard worn around the neck.
    o Tape a piece of masking tape on your wrist. Every time you observe the target behavior, put a checkmark on the masking tape. The number of checkmarks obtained can be transferred later to a data collection form.
    o Teach your student to monitor his or her own target behavior, if possible. Provide him or her with a data collection form; teach the student to recognize the target behavior and to put a checkmark in the correct place when the behavior occurs. Likewise, you can teach the student to self-reinforce him- or herself as part of the entire intervention procedure.
    o Have a classroom assistant or a paraeducator collect the data as part of his or her classroom duties.
- Graph the data. Remember that a picture is worth a thousand words. It is much easier for everyone to analyze the data if they can see its trend.

Finally, make sure that you do not simply engage in busy work when you collect data. Make it a priority to analyze the data and use the information to direct ongoing intervention. One useful approach is to establish frequent and regular meetings with team members for the purpose of discussing the data and the overall program for the student. You can find additional information on data collection in the section on behavior.

An Applied Behavior Analysis (ABA) Program

When working with students who are significantly delayed in a number of developmental areas and are falling far behind their peers, consider designing an intensive ABA program that includes DTT as well as contemporary ABA interventions, such as pivotal response training (PRT), that make use of the student's natural environment. Such a program tackles head-on the major problems facing students with autism: teaching them how to learn, increasing their motivation to participate in a wide variety of activities, addressing language delays, as well as teaching compliance and following routines. The clarity of instruction, the immediate feedback, and the emphasis on the student achieving success are all hallmarks of ABA that accelerate a student's learning.

When designing an ABA program decide first what behaviors or skills need to be taught by conducting a thorough assessment of the students' strengths and weaknesses. For an in-depth discussion of the assessment tools see Chapter 2. Once the assessment is complete, you will have a good idea about your students' needs. At this point, you are ready to choose a curriculum guide to follow. The guides that we have found most useful are described below.

The curriculum guides that cover all areas of development and which are easy to use in a school ABA program are as follows:

- *The Behavioral Interventions for Young Children With Autism: A Manual for Parents and Professionals* (Maurice, Green, & Luce, 1996) offers a beginning, an intermediate, and an advanced curriculum guide complete with detailed programs and data collection forms.
- *A Work in Progress: Behavior Management Strategies and a Curriculum for Intensive Behavioral Treatment of Autism* (Leaf & McEachin, 1999) is also a comprehensive curriculum guide with complete, detailed programs and data collection forms.

You may also design a program for your student based on the following tools:

- *The Assessment of Basic Language and Learning Skills* (ABLLS; Partington, 2006) lists the skills in all areas of development based on scope and sequence. In addition, it provides a visual representation for the teachers as the student progresses through these skills.
- *The Developmental Teaching Objectives for DTORF-R: For Assessment and Teaching Emotional Competence, Revised* (DTORF-R; Wood, Davis, Swindle, & Quirk, 1996) is another good resource for choosing objectives to teach our students with ASD. Like ABLLS, the DTORF-R lists skills based on scope and sequence in all areas of a student's development.

Once you have chosen your objectives, you will want to make sure you address the following questions:

- How are you going to teach them, how are you going to break down each objective (task analysis), how are you going to present the materials, what response are you requiring, how are you going to reinforce, what level of prompt are you going to use?
- When and where are you going to teach them? For purposes of generalization it is important to have various persons involved in teaching the student.
- How will the data be collected?

- What is the criterion for mastery, so that you know when a goal has been achieved? The criterion for mastery is usually 80% to 100% correct on three consecutive sessions.

An effective ABA program will also include the following components:

- A team member, assigned to be in charge of the student's program to ensure that there are always enough materials and supplies, graphs and analyzes the data and chooses new programs as old ones are mastered or moved to maintenance status.
- Objectives that target attending, imitation, academic, behavioral, communication/social, and self-help skills. Pay special attention to functional and age appropriate skills.
- A schedule with information on the individuals working with the student, the time, the location, and the objective/program at each time interval (see Figure 3.1).
- Visual supports for the student such as a visual schedule, pictorial representations of routines, tasks and reinforcers, and listing of specific expectations. For a more in-depth discussion, see Chapter 4.
- Choice making is incorporated as much as possible; allow your student to choose the order of activities or which activities to complete.
- Student's data and progress is reviewed on a regular basis.
- Persons implementing ABA should have on-going training and supervision.

For a more detailed discussion on how to design and organize the intervention program see Chapter 3.

We devoted this section to the principles and techniques of ABA because they are regarded as best-practice strategies for students with autism. As described above, these principles are equally effective in changing behaviors and teaching new skills in general education settings as they are in more restrictive environments. To achieve success, the special education staff joins forces with the general education teachers to creatively implement these principles. These techniques will prove effective not only for the students with autism, but they can also benefit other students in the classroom who may be also struggling.

Do you remember the binder—the organizational tool described in Chapter 3? Your students will probably advance quickly through some programs, and they might make slow progress in others. They might perform better for some teachers and not so well for others. Because time in schools is so limited, your binder will help ensure that all teachers know at all times how the student is performing, what programs he or she has mastered, and which ones still need to be taught. The binder will tell each teacher working with a student what skill he or she is working on, the level of performance, and any behavioral issues that might arise. The information collected in the binder can also be used to give parents immediate feedback on their child's progress or for writing periodic progress reports.

Remember Dan described in the vignette at the beginning of the chapter? The middle school principal formed a positive behavioral support team around Dan. The team quickly focused on the three main issues: (1) peeling skin off his hands, (2) failing grades because of organizational difficulties, and (3) slowness to answer questions. They assessed the function of the first behavior and concluded that Dan peeled the skin of his hands to relieve anxiety and for sensory input. As they considered his environment and the social expectations, they determined that changing classes each hour and having multiple teachers as well as the adolescent peer interaction were all very demanding. They reviewed his records and found documentation of slower processing time which would affect his ability to answer questions quickly. His organizational skills are yet another stressor.

The team chose the following interventions: (1) It provided a variety of fidgets for him to use when he felt the need to pick at his hands; (2) it designated the special education room as home base for Dan, and he was encouraged to go there to seek support from the special education teacher any time he felt anxious or overwhelmed; (3) it set up a folder system in the special education room for his English assignments and a paraeducator assigned to monitor it; and (4) the social worker and the speech-language pathologist worked with him to give him some phrases he could use, such as "Well, let me think," when he needed a little more time to answer a question. These supports reduced Dan's anxiety at school and improved his grades; the positive results encouraged the team to use the same approach for a number of other students who were struggling with organizational and anxiety issues.

Resource A

Psychological and Educational Assessment and Screening Tools

Screening and Diagnostic Tests

- *Asperger Syndrome Diagnostic Scale* (ASDS) (Myles, Bock, & Simpson, 2000). This standardized rating scale is quick and easy to use by anyone who knows the student well. In about 10 to 15 minutes, it can provide an Asperger syndrome (AS) quotient that indicates the likelihood of AS in students ages 5 through 18. The items cover cognitive, maladaptive, language, social, and sensorimotor development.
- *The Autism Diagnostic Interview, Revised* (ADI-R) (Lord, Rutter, & Le Couteur, 1994; Rutter, Le Couteur, & Lord, 2003), designed for students older than two years, is a structured interview containing four main factors: the student's communication, social interaction, repetitive behaviors, and age-of-onset symptoms. Because of the time needed to administer the ADI-R by clinically trained personnel (minimum of 90 minutes), it is often considered time consuming. Clinicians must be trained in the administration of this instrument.
- *Autism Diagnostic Observation Schedule* (ADOS) Wester Psychological Services (WPS) version (Lord, Rutter, DiLavore, & Risi, 2002) is a standardized assessment of social behavior in natural communicative contexts, as well as play or imaginative use of materials. It is used to evaluate a wide range of developmental levels: from students who are nonverbal to those with well developed language skills. It can be used with toddlers as well as with adults. Clinicians must be trained in the administration of this instrument.
- *Childhood Autism Rating Scale* (CARS) (Schopler, Reichler, & Renner, 1988) is designed to identify autism in children as young as two years of age. Scores falling within the autistic range are divided into two categories: mild-to-moderate and severe. Although accuracy is improved with experience, CARS can be administered by any professional who has had only minimal exposure to autism and was briefly trained to use this instrument. Additionally, two training videos showing how to use and score the scale are available from WPS.
- *Gilliam Autism Rating Scale, Second Edition* (GARS-2) (Gilliam, 2006), is a standardized instrument used in schools for students age 3 through 22 to determine the likelihood that a student has autism. This is a quick and easy instrument that takes between 5 and 10 minutes to be completed by any person who is familiar with the student.
- *Krug Asperger's Disorder Index* (KADI) (Krug & Arick, 2003) is a quick and easy instrument for screening AS. It is standardized for use with individuals 6 to 21 years of age.
- *Social Responsiveness Scale* (SRS) (Constantino & Gruber, 2005) is a rating scale for students 4 to 18 years of age that can be completed by a teacher or parent in 15 to 20 minutes. It measures social difficulties as they occur in the natural setting according to severity, thus allowing the rater to distinguish between students who have AS, pervasive developmental disorder not otherwise specified (PDD-NOS), autism, and schizoid personality disorder of childhood.

Intelligence Assessment Tests

- *Stanford-Binet Intelligence Scale, Fifth Edition* (SB5) (Roid, 2005), is an instrument that measures a person's cognitive abilities relative to other people of the same age group. An advantage of the SB5 is that the nonverbal portion has a wide variety of items which allows for better assessment of children with communication disorders.
- *Test of Nonverbal Intelligence 3* (TONI 3) (Brown, Sherbenou, & Johnsen, 1997) is a norm-referenced measure of intelligence, aptitude, abstract reasoning, and problem solving that is completely free of the use of language. The test requires no reading, writing, speaking, or listening on the part of the test subject. It is completely nonverbal and largely motor-free, requiring only a point, nod, or symbolic gesture to indicate response choices. It has norms for individuals 6 to 89 years of age and like its counterpart, the Universal Nonverbal Intelligence Test (UNIT) (Bracken & McCullum, 1998), does not take long to administer.
- *Universal Nonverbal Intelligence Test* (UNIT) (Bracken & McCullum, 1998) is an assessment of general intelligence for students from kindergarten through Grade 12 measured nonverbally. This test uses multiple response modes including manipulatives, paper and pencil, and pointing.
- *Wechsler Intelligence Scale for Children, Fourth Edition* (WISC-IV) (Wechsler, 2003), assesses the intelligence and cognitive abilities of children ages 6 through 16. This new edition consists of four sets of subtests: verbal comprehension index, perceptual reasoning index, working memory index, and processing speed index. In addition to providing a full scale intelligence quotient, the WISC-IV provides information on the learning style of the student.

Tests for Identifying Current Level of Performance and Educational Objectives

- *Adolescent and Adult Psychoeducational Profile* (AAPEP) (Mesibov, Schopler, Schaffer, & Landrus, 1988) provides a developmental approach to assessing students' strengths and deficits. This instrument is designed for students 12 years of age and older with moderate to severe disabilities, in areas such as vocational skills, independent functioning, leisure skills, functional communication, and interpersonal behavior. This tool is completed through direct observation and interaction with a student and can be completed by any professional familiar with autism spectrum disorders (ASD) characteristics. Just like *The Psychoeducational Profile, 3rd Edition* (PEP-3), the AAPEP can be a time-consuming endeavor depending on a student's behavior.
- *The Assessment of Basic Language and Learning Skills* (ABLLS-R) (Partington, 2006) is an assessment, curriculum guide, and skills tracking system for students with language delays. This instrument contains a task analysis of the many skills necessary to communicate successfully and to learn from everyday experiences. In addition, it provides a baseline of a student's current functioning in all areas of development: academics, social interaction, communication, behavior, and self-help skills. ABLLS can be completed by any professional familiar with the student. The information obtained from this instrument can help professionals develop effective individualized educational plans (IEPs), as well as track a student's progress in the acquisition of each skill.
- *Behavior Assessment Scale for Children, Second Edition* (BASC-2) (Reynolds & Kamphaus, 2004), provides a comprehensive system for measuring behavior and emotions in individuals 2 through 21 years of age. There are rating scales for teachers and parents as well as a self-report of personality and a student observation form. This instrument is a multi-method, multidimensional system that allows you to look at a student's history, focus

on current behavior, self-perceptions, and emotions in the domains of behavior, personality, and development. Although it does not diagnose ASD, BASC can assist in evaluating behavioral aspects that may impact students with ASD (e.g., anxiety disorder, Attention Deficit Disorder). It is necessary to have a PhD in Psychology or be a certified School Psychologist to administer this instrument.

- *Developmental Teaching Objectives Rating Form, Revised* (DTORF-R) (Wood, Davis, Swindle, & Quirk, 1996), is a checklist that can be completed relatively quickly by the student's teacher and is designed to collect information on the student's cognitive, behavioral, communication, and social skills from birth through age 16. The teacher will use the results to identify students in need of referral for special help, to make placement decisions, to identify instructional objectives, and to document progress in all developmental areas. This tool allows you to track progress for all your students in the class on one form.

- *Psychoeducational Profile, Third Edition* (PEP-3) (Schopler, Lansing, Reichler, & Marcus, 2005), offers a developmental approach to the assessment of students with ASD or related developmental disorders. This tool is an inventory of behaviors and skills designed to identify uneven and idiosyncratic learning patterns of students with developmental age between 6 months and 7 years. The PEP-3 provides scores in communication, motor, and maladaptive behaviors along with performance subtests in cognitive verbal/preverbal, expressive language, receptive language, fine motor, gross motor, visual motor imitation, affective expression, social reciprocity, characteristic motor behaviors, and characteristic verbal behaviors. This instrument can help you compare your student's developmental level with a normative group of children in the autism spectrum as well as a group of children without autism.

- *Vineland Adaptive Behavior Scale* (VABS) (Sparrow, Cicchetti, & Balla, 2005) is a norm-referenced test designed to assess an individual's communication, daily living skills, socialization, and motor abilities. It does well in predicting a diagnosis of autism or AS and in discriminating between the two. For example, compared to students with high-functioning autism, individuals with AS will typically show higher abilities in communication but lower motor skill levels. VABS results can also be used to identify educational objectives for promoting functional skills. An advantage of using this instrument is that any professional or caregiver familiar with the student can complete it.

- *Woodcock-Johnson III* (WJ III) (Woodcock, McGrew, & Mather, 2001) is a comprehensive diagnostic tool for individuals of all ages, and it is used by evaluators to assess a student's cognitive and academic abilities and to determine whether a student has learning disabilities.

Communication Tests

- *Assessment of Social and Communication Skills for Children With Autism* (Quill, 2000) can assist the speech-language pathologist (SLP) in the evaluation of a wide range of social and communication abilities of students with autism. With this instrument you gather information about behaviors that are ritualistic, nonverbal social interaction skills, imitation skills, organizational skills, solitary play skills, social play skills, group skills, community social skills, basic communicative functions, socioemotional skills, and basic conversational skills. This tool can easily be used to develop a student's IEP and to monitor his or her progress in the areas of social and communication skills.

- *Clinical Evaluation of Language Fundamentals, Fourth Edition* (CELF-4) (Semel, Wiig, & Secord, 2003), is a norm-referenced comprehensive assessment that evaluates language and determines whether or not a language disorder is present by administering four subtests. It takes approximately 30 to 45 minutes to complete the four subtests for the core language score. There are a total of 18 subtests that cover content, structure, and use of language and can be used with students ages 5 to 21.

- *Test of Pragmatic Language, Second Edition* (TOPL-2) (Phelps-Terasaki & Phelps-Gunn, 2007), is norm-referenced and designed to assess the pragmatic language skills of students ages 6 to 18 years. The test takes between 45 minutes to an hour to administer and covers the six core areas of physical setting, audience, topic, purpose, visual-gestural cues, and abstraction. This instrument allows you to assess the student's strengths and weaknesses as well as document progress.
- *Test of Problem Solving–Elementary, Revised* (TOPS-E) (Bowers, Huisingh, & LoGiudice, 2005), is a particularly useful assessment tool for uncovering the range of communication difficulties encountered by even the highly verbal students with ASD. TOPS pinpoints the specific difficulties these students have predicting outcomes, problem solving, determining solutions, drawing inferences, empathizing, using context cues, and vocabulary comprehension.
- *Test of Problem Solving 2–Adolescent* (TOPS 2-Adolescent) (Bowers, Huisingh, Barrett, Orman, & LoGuidice, 2007) is designed to assess critical and affective thinking skills for students ages 12 through 17. Both versions of TOPS are useful in that they will show the student's ability to use language to think.

Sensory Tests

- *Sensory Profile* (Dunn, 1999) is a questionnaire that can be used with children ages 3 to 10 to determine how well they process sensory information in everyday situations. This instrument will also profile the sensory system's effect on functional performance.
- *Adolescent/Adult Sensory Profile* (Brown & Dunn, 2002) is a self-questionnaire that enables individuals to evaluate themselves and how their sensory processing affects their daily performance patterns.
- *Sensory Processing Measure–Home Form* (SPM) (Parham, Ecker, Miller-Kuhaneck, Henry, & Glennon, 2007) and *Main Classroom and School Environment Forms* (Miller-Kuhaneck, Henry, Glennon, & Mu, 2007) are designed to assess children kindergarten through 6th grade (ages 5 to 12). The test items cover a wide range of behaviors and characteristics related to sensory processing, social participation, and praxis. The home form and the main classroom form each yield norm-referenced standard scores in the areas of vision, hearing, touch, body awareness, balance and motion, planning and ideas, and total sensory systems.

Resource B

The Binder

The binder includes	Done
1. Student's IEP, including medical plan, dietary restrictions, and behavior plan, if applicable	
2. Student's daily schedule, including sensory breaks	
3. Classroom objectives form	

4. Programs
 	
• A list of the relevant programs. Each program should be separated by a labeled divider and should include the following:
  ○ A student's specific objective for each program
  ○ Data collection form
  ○ Graphs
  ○ Plastic pockets along with each program when needed to hold relevant materials (e.g., cards)
  ○ Small paper clips to close pockets	

5. Home-school communication forms	
6. Regular team meetings minutes	
7. Extra blank forms—always keep a good supply of extra forms such as the following: • Reinforcement assessment forms • Generic data forms • Graphs • Classroom objectives • Behavior intervention data collection form • Behavior intervention form	

Copyright © 2009 by Corwin. All rights reserved. Reprinted from *The Educator's Guide to Teaching Students With Autism Spectrum Disorders*, by Josefa Ben-Arieh and Helen J. Miller. Thousand Oaks, CA: Corwin, www.corwinpress.com. Reproduction authorized only for the local school site or nonprofit organization that has purchased this book.

Resource C

Daily Schedules

Form 1

Student's name: _____   Date: _____

Daily Schedule

Time	Place	Person					Activities and Goals
		Monday	Tuesday	Wednesday	Thursday	Friday	

Copyright © 2009 by Corwin. All rights reserved. Reprinted from *The Educator's Guide to Teaching Students With Autism Spectrum Disorders*, by Josefa Ben-Arieh and Helen J. Miller. Thousand Oaks, CA: Corwin, www.corwinpress.com. Reproduction authorized only for the local school site or nonprofit organization that has purchased this book.

Form 2

Student's name: _____   Date: _____

Daily Schedule

Time	Place	Goals

Copyright © 2009 by Corwin. All rights reserved. Reprinted from *The Educator's Guide to Teaching Students With Autism Spectrum Disorders,* by Josefa Ben-Arieh and Helen J. Miller. Thousand Oaks, CA: Corwin, www.corwinpress.com. Reproduction authorized only for the local school site or nonprofit organization that has purchased this book.

Resource D

A Student's Classroom Objectives

Student's name: _____   Date: _____

Classroom Objectives

Sociocommunicative Goals	Monday	Tuesday	Wednesday	Thursday	Friday
_____					
_____					
_____					
_____					

Behavioral Goals	Monday	Tuesday	Wednesday	Thursday	Friday
_____					
_____					
_____					
_____					

Other Goals	Monday	Tuesday	Wednesday	Thursday	Friday
_____					
_____					
_____					
_____					

Note: Score each day a "+" if the student performs the skill independently or to established criterion and score a "−" if he or she does not.

Copyright © 2009 by Corwin. All rights reserved. Reprinted from *The Educator's Guide to Teaching Students With Autism Spectrum Disorders,* by Josefa Ben-Arieh and Helen J. Miller. Thousand Oaks, CA: Corwin, www.corwinpress.com. Reproduction authorized only for the local school site or nonprofit organization that has purchased this book.

Resource E

Data Collection Forms

Data and Graph Collection Form

Student's name: _____ Objective: _____

Date																						
+10																							100%
+9																							90%
+8																							80%
+7																							70%
+6																							60%
+5																							50%
+4																							40%
+3																							30%
+2																							20%
+1																							10%
−1																							−1
−2																							−2
−3																							−3
−4																							−4
−5																							−5
−6																							−6
−7																							−7
−8																							−8
−9																							−9
−10																							−10

Note: Each teaching session should be recorded in one vertical column. If the student's response is correct, mark an X in the higher half of the graph, starting with +1. If the student's response is incorrect or fails to respond, mark an X starting with −1. By connecting the squares on the top half of this form, you will automatically create a graph showing percentage correct for each teaching session. **This graph works if you do 10 trials a session.**

Copyright © 2009 by Corwin. All rights reserved. Reprinted from *The Educator's Guide to Teaching Students With Autism Spectrum Disorders*, by Josefa Ben-Arieh and Helen J. Miller. Thousand Oaks, CA: Corwin, www.corwinpress.com. Reproduction authorized only for the local school site or nonprofit organization that has purchased this book.

Data Probe Form

Student's name: _____

Objective	Date				
1.					
2.					
3.					
4.					
5.					
6.					
7.					
8.					
9.					
10.					
Percentage Correct					

Note: Use this form at the beginning of every teaching session to determine what to teach. Use it either to take data on 5 items twice or on 10 items. + for correct; − for incorrect or lack of response

Copyright © 2009 by Corwin. All rights reserved. Reprinted from *The Educator's Guide to Teaching Students With Autism Spectrum Disorders*, by Josefa Ben-Arieh and Helen J. Miller. Thousand Oaks, CA: Corwin, www.corwinpress.com. Reproduction authorized only for the local school site or nonprofit organization that has purchased this book.

Data Collection Form for JARs

Receptive Understanding of Directions

Score + if student responds correctly without prompts.
Score – if student does not respond correctly or fails to respond.

Date: _____

Educator's name: _____

Receptive Instructions						% Correct
1.						
2.						
3.						
4.						
5.						

Date: _____

Educator's name: _____

Receptive Instructions						% Correct
1.						
2.						
3.						
4.						
5.						

Copyright © 2009 by Corwin. All rights reserved. Reprinted from *The Educator's Guide to Teaching Students With Autism Spectrum Disorders*, by Josefa Ben-Arieh and Helen J. Miller. Thousand Oaks, CA: Corwin, www.corwinpress.com. Reproduction authorized only for the local school site or nonprofit organization that has purchased this book.

Data Graphing Form

Student's name: _____

Target behavior: _____ Start Date: _____

100																													
90																													
80																													
70																													
60																													
50																													
40																													
30																													
20																													
10																													
0																													
day																													

Target behavior: _____ Start Date: _____

100																													
90																													
80																													
70																													
60																													
50																													
40																													
30																													
20																													
10																													
0																													
day																													

Copyright © 2009 by Corwin. All rights reserved. Reprinted from *The Educator's Guide to Teaching Students With Autism Spectrum Disorders*, by Josefa Ben-Arieh and Helen J. Miller. Thousand Oaks, CA: Corwin, www.corwinpress.com. Reproduction authorized only for the local school site or nonprofit organization that has purchased this book.

Data Collection Form for JARs

Expressive Exchanges

Score + if student's verbal interaction meets criterion independently.
Score − if student's verbal interaction does not meet criterion independently.

Date: _____

Educator's name: _____

Verbal utterance						% Correct
1.						
2.						
3.						
4.						
5.						

Date: _____

Educator's name: _____

Verbal utterance						% Correct
1.						
2.						
3.						
4.						
5.						

Copyright © 2009 by Corwin. All rights reserved. Reprinted from *The Educator's Guide to Teaching Students With Autism Spectrum Disorders,* by Josefa Ben-Arieh and Helen J. Miller. Thousand Oaks, CA: Corwin, www.corwinpress.com. Reproduction authorized only for the local school site or nonprofit organization that has purchased this book.

Behavior Data Collection Form

Frequency

Student's name: _____

Date: _____

Activity/Class: _____

Behavior: _____

Behavior	Date	1	2	3	4	5	6	7	8	9	10	11	12	13	14	15	16	17	18	19	20	Total

Copyright © 2009 by Corwin. All rights reserved. Reprinted from *The Educator's Guide to Teaching Students With Autism Spectrum Disorders*, by Josefa Ben-Arieh and Helen J. Miller.

Behavior Data Collection Form

Time Sampling Recording

Student's name: _____

Date: _____

Activity/Class: _____

Behavior: _____

2 min.	4 min.	6 min.	8 min.	10 min.	12 min.	14 min.	16 min.	18 min.	20 min.

Copyright © 2009 by Corwin. All rights reserved. Reprinted from *The Educator's Guide to Teaching Students With Autism Spectrum Disorders*, by Josefa Ben-Arieh and Helen J. Miller. Thousand Oaks, CA: Corwin, www.corwinpress.com. Reproduction authorized only for the local school site or nonprofit organization that has purchased this book.

Behavior Data Form

Student's name: _____

Data collectors' names: _____

Behavior: _____ (the behavior must be measurable)

Date	Duration	Setting/Activity	Antecedent	Consequences
	Start: _____ End: _____			
	Start: _____ End: _____			
	Start: _____ End: _____			
	Start: _____ End: _____			
	Start: _____ End: _____			
	Start: _____ End: _____			
	Start: _____ End: _____			
	Start: _____ End: _____			
	Start: _____ End: _____			

Copyright © 2009 by Corwin. All rights reserved. Reprinted from *The Educator's Guide to Teaching Students With Autism Spectrum Disorders*, by Josefa Ben-Arieh and Helen J. Miller. Thousand Oaks, CA: Corwin, www.corwinpress.com. Reproduction authorized only for the local school site or nonprofit organization that has purchased this book.

Resource F

Teacher–Parent Communication Forms

Form 1

Name: _____   Date: _____

Rating scale: 1 (great difficulty), 2 (some difficulty), 3 (good), 4 (great), 5 (fantastic)

Circle time:
1   2   3   4   5
Worked on: _____

Free play/center time:
1   2   3   4   5
Worked on: _____

Outside time:
1   2   3   4   5
Worked on: _____

One-on-one work time:
1   2   3   4   5
Worked on: _____

Specials (OT, PT, SLP):
1   2   3   4   5
Worked on: _____

Communication:
1   2   3   4   5
Worked on: _____

_____
_____
_____
_____
_____
_____
_____
_____
_____
_____

Parents' response: _____
_____
_____
_____

Copyright © 2009 by Corwin. All rights reserved. Reprinted from *The Educator's Guide to Teaching Students With Autism Spectrum Disorders,* by Josefa Ben-Arieh and Helen J. Miller. Thousand Oaks, CA: Corwin, www.corwinpress.com. Reproduction authorized only for the local school site or nonprofit organization that has purchased this book.

Form 2

My Day at School

What did you do in school today?

I_____.

Who did you play with?

I played with _____. _____*is my friend.*

Was anyone absent today?

_____.

What did you eat for lunch?

I ate _____ *and* _____. *I drank* _____.

What one thing did you learn in school today?

Today I learned _____.

Note: Teacher helps student fill out this form. Student's answers are in italics.

Copyright © 2009 by Corwin. All rights reserved. Reprinted from *The Educator's Guide to Teaching Students With Autism Spectrum Disorders*, by Josefa Ben-Arieh and Helen J. Miller. Thousand Oaks, CA: Corwin, www.corwinpress.com. Reproduction authorized only for the local school site or nonprofit organization that has purchased this book.

Resource G

Team Meeting Minutes

Student's name: _____   Date: _____

Participants:

Agenda:

Discussion:

Responsibilities and Timeline:

Date Due	Person Responsible	Action	Completed

Note: Each team member receives a copy after the meeting.

Copyright © 2009 by Corwin. All rights reserved. Reprinted from *The Educator's Guide to Teaching Students With Autism Spectrum Disorders,* by Josefa Ben-Arieh and Helen J. Miller. Thousand Oaks, CA: Corwin, www.corwinpress.com. Reproduction authorized only for the local school site or nonprofit organization that has purchased this book.

Resource H

Functional Analysis Screening Tool (FAST)

Client: _____   Date: _____

Informant: _____   Interviewer: _____

To the Interviewer: The FAST identifies environmental and physical factors that may influence problem behaviors. It should be used only for screening purposes as part of a comprehensive functional analysis of the behavior. Administer the FAST to several individuals who interact with the client frequently. Then use the results as a guide for conducting a series of direct observations in different situations to verify behavioral functions and to identify other factors that may influence the problem behavior.

To the Informant: Complete the sections below. Then read each question carefully and answer it by circling "Yes" or "No." If you are uncertain about an answer, circle "N/A."

Informant-Client Relationship

1. Indicate your relationship to the person: ___ Parent ___ Instructor ___ Therapist/Residential Staff ___ (Other)

2. How long have you known the person? ___ Years ____ Months

3. Do you interact with the person daily? ____ Yes ____ No

4. In what situations do you usually interact with the person?
   ___ Meals ___ Academic training
   ___ Leisure ___ Work or vocational training
   ___ Self-care _____ (Other)

Problem Behavior Information

1. Problem behavior (check and describe):
   __ Aggression _____
   __ Self-Injury _____
   __ Stereotypy _____
   __ Property destruction _____
   __ Other _____

2. Frequency: __ Hourly __ Daily __ Weekly __ Less often

3. Severity:
   __ Mild: Disruptive but little risk to property or health
   __ Moderate: Property damage or minor injury
   __ Severe: Significant threat to health or safety

4. Situations in which the problem behavior is *most* likely:

Days/times _____

Settings/activities _____

Persons present _____

5. Situations in which the problem behavior is *least* likely:

Days/times _____

Settings/activities _____

Persons present _____

6. What is usually happening to the person right *before* the problem behavior occurs?

_____

_____

7. What usually happens to the person right *after* the problem behavior occurs?

_____

_____

8. Current treatments _____

_____

_____

_____

_____

_____

———————— ✀ ————————

1.	Does the person usually engage in the problem behavior when (s)he is being ignored or when caregivers are paying attention to someone else?	Yes	No	N/A
2.	Does the person usually engage in the problem behavior when requests for preferred activities (games, snacks) are denied or when these items are taken away?	Yes	No	N/A
3.	When the problem behavior occurs, do you or other caregivers usually try to calm the person down or try to engage the person in preferred activities?	Yes	No	N/A
4.	Is the person usually well behaved when (s)he is getting lots of attention or when preferred items or activities are freely available?	Yes	No	N/A
5.	Is the person resistant when asked to perform a task or to participate in group activities?	Yes	No	N/A
6.	Does the person usually engage in the problem behavior when asked to perform a task or to participate in group activities?	Yes	No	N/A
7.	When the problem behavior occurs, is the person usually given a break from tasks?	Yes	No	N/A
8.	Is the person usually well behaved when (s)he is not required to do anything?	Yes	No	N/A

9.	Does the problem behavior seem to be a "ritual" or habit, repeatedly occurring the same way?	Yes	No	N/A
10.	Does the person usually engage in the problem behavior even when no one is around or watching?	Yes	No	N/A
11.	Does the person prefer engaging in the problem behavior over other types of leisure activities?	Yes	No	N/A
12.	Does the problem behavior appear to provide some sort of "sensory stimulation?"	Yes	No	N/A
13.	Does the person usually engage in the problem behavior more often when (s)he is ill?	Yes	No	N/A
14.	Is the problem behavior cyclical, occurring at high rates for several days and then stopping?	Yes	No	N/A
15.	Does the person have recurrent painful conditions such as ear infections or allergies? If so, please list_____	Yes	No	N/A
16.	If the person is experiencing physical problems, and these are treated, does the problem behavior usually go away?	Yes	No	N/A

Scoring Summary

Circle the number of each question that was answered "Yes."

Items Circled "Yes"				Total	Potential Source of Reinforcement
1	2	3	4	____	Social (attention/preferred items)
5	6	7	8	____	Social (escape)
9	10	11	12	____	Automatic (sensory stimulation)
13	14	15	16	____	Automatic (pain attenuation)

Source: © 2002 The Florida Center on Self-Injury. From H. L. Goh, B. A. Iwata, & I. G. DeLeon, *Functional Analysis Screening Tool (FAST)* (Gainesville, FL: The Florida Center on Self-Injury, 2002).

Resource I

A Behavior Intervention Plan (BIP)

Date: _____

Student name: _____   Main implementer: _____

Behavior	Expected Outcome(s)/ Goal(s)	Positive Supports and Intervention(s)	Implementers	Intervention Review

Copyright © 2009 by Corwin. All rights reserved. Reprinted from *The Educator's Guide to Teaching Students With Autism Spectrum Disorders*, by Josefa Ben-Arieh and Helen J. Miller. Thousand Oaks, CA: Corwin, www.corwinpress.com. Reproduction authorized only for the local school site or nonprofit organization that has purchased this book.

Resource J

Letter of Permission to Participate in the Circle of Friends

Date: _____

Dear Parents,

Circle of Friends is a program for students to work on peer relationships and on making friends. It consists of a small group of classroom peers who meet with a facilitator on a weekly basis. During Circle of Friends the students learn to respect and support each other throughout the day. For 20 to 30 minutes the facilitator assists the students in discussing any problems from the previous week, coming up with suggestions on ways to correct them, and encouraging friendship skills while participating in an activity such as playing a board game.

We are forming a Circle of Friends group for students in _____ class. It will meet approximately once a week at lunch time.

_____ suggested that your child would be an asset to the group. Participation, of course, is voluntary, but I would be very pleased if you and your child would agree to participate in this activity for at least a month. Typically, all students in the group benefit and show an increased level of empathy as well as an enhanced sense of competence and pride.

Please call me if you have any questions. Please sign and return the permission slip below if you agree to your child's participation.

Thank you,

I give permission for _____ (child's name) to participate in Circle of Friends _____ (parent signature) _____ (date).

Copyright © 2009 by Corwin. All rights reserved. Reprinted from *The Educator's Guide to Teaching Students With Autism Spectrum Disorders,* by Josefa Ben-Arieh and Helen J. Miller. Thousand Oaks, CA: Corwin, www.corwinpress.com. Reproduction authorized only for the local school site or nonprofit organization that has purchased this book.

Resource K

A Reinforcement Chart

I am working for _____.

Copyright © 2009 by Corwin. All rights reserved. Reprinted from *The Educator's Guide to Teaching Students With Autism Spectrum Disorders*, by Josefa Ben-Arieh and Helen J. Miller. Thousand Oaks, CA: Corwin, www.corwinpress.com. Reproduction authorized only for the local school site or nonprofit organization that has purchased this book.

Appendix A

Guidelines for Administrators

As an administrator responsible for students in the autism spectrum, you will be keenly aware of the challenges they face in the school setting. These students are easily misunderstood and the intensity and complexity of their needs, and ensuing behaviors, will call for unique interventions.

One of the most important first steps you can take is to make sure that your entire staff is well-informed on what it means to be in the autism spectrum. Without an understanding of how students with autism perceive the world, adults tend to interpret their inappropriate behavior as manipulative. This may well result in patterns of interaction between staff and student that exacerbate the problems our students face. Ongoing support and training from professionals who are well versed in autism is a must. Second, as administrator, you will play a decisive role in teacher assignments, environmental supports, approving modifications for field trips, and assembly attendance, as well as the allocation of paraeducators and other staff support. You can foster a culture of acceptance in your school for students in the spectrum by encouraging staff to meet regularly together and with parents to discuss interventions that can assist the student both academically and socially. Here are some suggestions or guidelines to keep in mind as you work with staff, parents, and their student in the autism spectrum.

Classroom and Teacher Assignments

When making teacher assignments, remember that the teacher who does best with students with autism spectrum disorder (ASD) tends to have the following characteristics:

- A structured yet flexible management style
- Gives instructions clearly and accompanies them with a visual model
- Has a written schedule on the board
- Follows consistent classroom routines and expectations for student behavior
- Is warm and welcoming to students who do not fit the norm
- Uses positive behavioral supports rather than a punitive approach
- Is confident in his or her teaching skills, but also feels comfortable asking for advice and support and is open to receiving suggestions from parents and support personnel

School Environment

Students with ASD are often affected by their environment. The following are important considerations:

- The student may be stressed by noise, so
  - speak softly,
  - warn them when there might be a loud noise,
  - seat them away from air conditioning units and any computers, and
  - pay attention to them when they complain about slight noises other students might be making such as tapping on the desk.
- The student may be sensitive to fluorescent lighting or bright lighting, so consider
  - turning off the lights or dimming them,
  - changing the color to soften the effect,
  - using bulbs that do not flicker, and
  - having the student wear sunglasses.
- The student may be affected by his or her seating assignment, so
  - seat the student away from the main traffic flow area and in a location where he or she will not be frequently bumped by other students,
  - place the student at the end of an aisle and close to the front of the class, and
  - seat them beside students who are good role models, who have a caring spirit and are willing to help.
- The lunchroom with students sitting close together along with the smells and noise level may present a tremendous sensory and social challenge for the student with ASD, so
  - seat the student in a less busy section of the lunchroom,
  - find another location for the student to have lunch (e.g., the special education resource room or the principal's office), and
  - allow the student to arrive ahead of his or her peers and leave as soon as he or she is finished eating.
- Assemblies and field trips can be difficult because they are a change in schedule, may be overstimulating, and they usually have different formats and vary in length, so
  - prepare the student for the assembly by telling him or her a day in advance when it will be, how long it will last, and what will be expected of the student;
  - remind the teacher to list it on his or her daily schedule;
  - inform the teacher of the details at least a week in advance so he or she can write a social story; and
  - there are times when it is best to excuse the student from assemblies.
- Tornado and fire drills can be alarming, so
  - tell the teachers ahead of time when there will be an alarm sounded for the purpose of fire or tornado drill,
  - consider just announcing the drill over the loud speaker rather than sounding the alarm, and
  - allow for the teacher to take the student out ahead of time if you are going to sound the alarm so that they are less stressed.

It would be well worth the effort to put special covers on the fire alarms so that it is less likely that the student with ASD will pull the alarm (applies to a young student with developmental delays).

Special Considerations

Students in the autism spectrum often have unusual sleep and eating patterns. It is important to remind the staff that these are complex issues over which parents often have little control. However, parents need to be encouraged to seek medical advice.

Parents

Parents of children with autism often face undeserved criticism for their child's behaviors. However, parents cannot control the behaviors that occur at school. They cannot eliminate the sensory needs, the anxiety and depression, or the sociocommunicative delays that may lead to undesirable behaviors in their children. Parents are fully aware that their children may make life difficult for the school, but at the same time, they need to count on the professionalism of the school staff. It is important, therefore, for you to model a no-blame attitude toward the student and his or her family. If the student comes to school in the same clothes day after day, has not showered or combed his or her hair, remember that parents have to pick their battles—as do you! Instead of criticizing the parents or student, it is more helpful to join forces with them as you work to implement positive behavioral support strategies to change the undesirable behaviors.

Safety

The safety of both the student and the staff is, of course, a priority. The following supports should, therefore, be considered:

- Cell phone or two-way radio system for the teacher to call for back-up assistance especially when outside the building or isolated from other staff members.
- When the student is a flight risk, fencing around the playground may help as well as continual paraeducator or teacher support.
- Specialized training in how to assist the student, especially if restraint is involved.
- If a student needs a medical plan, it must be updated at least annually and kept in an easily accessible spot in the classroom.
- A quiet area, or home base, where the student can go to calm down and regulate his emotions when upset.

Teacher Professional Development

Teachers should be encouraged to learn about the characteristics of autism and research-based interventions such as those described in this book.

Staff Collaboration

Effective staff collaboration depends on regular meeting times when team members, including parents, can give their undivided attention to the student. It need not be a long period of time, 30 minutes may often suffice, but it does need to be a regularly scheduled meeting time. Twice a month is often a good starting point and this can be increased or decreased depending on the need.

Paraeducator Support

Students with ASD often require paraeducator support. When hiring a paraeducator to work with a student with autism, it is helpful to look for the following characteristics:

- Gentle and warm personality
- Consistent and organized
- Flexible and willing to be guided
- Soft spoken and yet firm
- Takes responsibility for teaching the student and does not blame the student
- Has a sense of humor

Maintaining a Positive School Climate

When students are disruptive or are failing to learn, your positive leadership role becomes crucial.

- The student's disruptive behaviors are a signal that there is a problem and must be seen as an impetus to reassess the environment, the academic demands, and all the supports—social, academic, behavioral, and sensory.
- Schedule short team meetings every other week to review current strategies and to plan for the coming week (consider using the team meeting form in this book); make sure they do not become gripe sessions but keep them focused on aspects of behavior the school can influence.
- Affirm both student and staff on a daily basis regardless of how tough the day.

Our students with ASD often make tremendous progress when the needed supports and interventions are in place. It is good to remember that all the effort and time put into creating the most beneficial program for students with ASD will almost always be beneficial to other students along the way.

Appendix B

Guidelines for Teachers and Support Staff

How to Be an Effective Team Player

There is no doubt that teaming for students with autism is essential. Because time is a scarce commodity in the schools, it is important to be as organized and intentional as possible when spending time discussing these difficult students. Teachers and support staff often spend a great deal of time talking about a student, but it does not result in a greater understanding of who is going to do what to help the student.

Here are some suggestions that really work:

- Find a time once every two weeks to meet as a team to talk about the student (this will eliminate the need for the teacher to discuss the different issues individually with team members, and it allows for the team members to get everybody's input at the same time).
- Keep the meetings to 30 minutes.
- At the start of the meeting, assign one member to take notes.
- Begin the meeting by gathering agenda items to discuss.
- Prioritize the agenda items because you only have 30 minutes. What does not get discussed will head up the agenda at the next meeting time.
- Discuss each topic, making sure to record facts, concerns, and intervention decisions that are made.

This format brings a focus to the meeting and you will find a lot gets accomplished in this time.

Importance of a Positive Attitude

Support staff can come alongside the other teaching staff to encourage them and to promote a "can do" attitude toward improving the student's behaviors.

Importance of Training

If possible go to specific autism trainings as a team. If only one team member can attend, make a point of having the information disseminated to other team members. Teaching students with autism spectrum disorder (ASD) requires a very different set of skills from those you use with other students on your caseload. It is important to see this as an opportunity to expand your expertise rather than feel defensive. Many support staff feel intimidated at first, but once they become familiar with the students and their specific needs and have received training in autism and appropriate interventions, they enjoy the challenge.

Importance of Data Collection

Because our students with ASD need very careful programming to be successful, it is necessary for the support staff to collect data on a regular basis to guide interventions. If you do not see progress, it is a signal that you should try a different intervention strategy or simplify the task. If you do not take data, you really have no way of gauging the effectiveness of your interventions, and you may be wasting everyone's time.

Importance of Communicating With Families

Parents are eager to get updates and suggestions from those working with their child. So, it is wise to set up regular times to visit with parents or to maintain a regular communication system. Parents have a wealth of information about their child that will be helpful to you, but do not count on them being able to solve problems you have at school. In fact, they may need your help to figure out solutions to difficulties they have at home. Because students with ASD often need help generalizing skills to new settings and new people, you will want to keep the parents abreast of the gains you make so that they can help establish them even further through practice outside of school.

References

Alberto, P. A., & Troutman, A. C. (2008). *Applied behavior analysis for teachers* (8th ed.). Upper Saddle River, NJ: Prentice Hall.

American Psychiatric Association. (2000). *Diagnostic and statistical manual of mental disorders* (4th ed.). Washington, DC: Author.

Anderson, J. (1998). *Sensory motor issues in autism* (2nd ed.). San Antonio, TX: Psychological Corporation.

Anderson, S., Taras, M., & Cannon, B. (1996). Teaching new skills to young children with autism. In C. Maurice, G. Green, & S. Luce (Eds.), *Behavioral interventions for young children with autism* (pp. 181–194). Austin, TX: PRO-ED.

Anzalone, M., & Williamson, G. G. (2000). Sensory processing and motor performance in autism spectrum disorders. In A. M. Wetherby & B. M. Prizant (Eds.), *Autism spectrum disorders: A transactional developmental perspective* (pp. 143–166). Baltimore: Paul H. Brookes.

Asperger, H. (1944). Die "Autistischen psychopathen" im kindsalter [Autism psychopathy in children]. *Archiv für Psychiatrie und Nervenkrankheiten, 117*, 76–136.

Attwood, T. (1998). *Asperger's syndrome: A guide for parents and professionals*. London: Jessica Kingsley.

Baron-Cohen, S. (1989). The autistic child's theory of mind: A case of specific developmental delay. *Journal of Child Psychology and Psychiatry, 30*(9), 285–297.

Baron-Cohen, S. (1992). Out of sight or out of mind: Another look at deception in autism. *Journal of Child Psychology and Psychiatry, 33*, 1141–1155.

Baron-Cohen, S. (2001). Reading the mind in the eyes test. *Journal of Developmental and Learning Disorders. 5*, 47–78.

Baron-Cohen, S., & Goodhart, F. (1994). The 'seeing leads to knowing' deficit in autism: The Pratt and Bryant probe. *British Journal of Developmental Psychology, 12*, 397–402.

Baron-Cohen, S., Leslie, A. M., & Frith, U. (1985). Does the autistic child have a "theory of mind"? *Cognition, 21*, 37–46.

Baron-Cohen, S., O'Riordan, M., Stone, V., Jones, R., & Plaisted, K. (1999). A new test of social sensitivity: Detection of faux pas in normal children and children with Asperger syndrome. *Journal of Autism and Developmental Disorders, 29*, 407–418.

Baron-Cohen, S., & Swettenham, J. (1997). The theory of mind hypothesis of autism: Relationship to executive function and central coherence. In D. J. Cohen & F. R. Volkmar (Eds.), *Handbook of autism and pervasive developmental disorders* (2nd ed., pp. 880–893). New York: John Wiley & Sons.

Bellini, S. (2006). *Building social relationships: A systematic approach to teaching social interaction skills to children and adolescents with autism spectrum disorders and other social difficulties*. Shawnee Mission, KS: Autism Asperger.

Bondy A., & Frost, L. (1994). The picture exchange communication system. *Focus on Autistic Behavior, 9*(3), 1–19.

Bowers, L., Huisingh, R., Barrett, M., Orman, J., & LoGiudice, C. (2007). *Test of problem solving— adolescent*. East Moline, IL: LinguiSystems.

Bowers, L., Huisingh, R., & LoGiudice, C. (2005). *Test of problem solving 3—elementary*. East Moline, IL: LinguiSystems.

Bracken, B. A., & McCullum, R. S. (1998). *The universal nonverbal intelligence test*. Chicago: Riverside.

Brown, C., & Dunn, W. (2002). *Adolescent/Adult sensory profile manual*. San Antonio, TX: Harcourt Assessment.

Brown, K. E., & Mirenda, P. (2006). Contingency mapping: Use of a novel visual support strategy as an adjunct to functional equivalence training. *Journal of Positive Behavior Interventions, 8*(3), 155–164.

Brown, L., Sherbenou, R., & Johnsen, S. (1997). *Test of nonverbal intelligence* (3rd ed.). Austin, TX: PRO-ED.

Buron, K. D., & Curtis, M. (2003). *The incredible 5-point scale.* Shawnee Mission, KS: Autism Asperger.

Cafiero, J. (1998). Communication power for individuals with autism. *Focus on Autism and Other Developmental Disabilities, 13*(2), 113–121.

Charlop, M., & Milstein, J. (1989). Teaching autistic children conversational speech using video modeling. *Journal of Applied Behavioral Analysis, 22,* 275–285.

Constantino, J. N., & Gruber, C. P. (2005). *Social Responsiveness Scale.* Los Angeles: Western Psychological Services.

Department of Health and Human Services Centers for Disease Control and Prevention (CDC). (2007, February 8). *CDC releases new data on autism spectrum disorders (ASDs) from multiple communities in the United States.* Retrieved February 8, 2007, from http://www.cdc.gov/media/pressrel/2007/r070208.htm?s_cid=mediarel_r070208

Dewey, M. (1998). Living with Asperger's syndrome. In U. Frith (Ed.), *Autism and Asperger syndrome.* Cambridge, UK: Cambridge University Press.

Dunn, W. (1999). *The sensory profile.* San Antonio, TX: Psychological Corp.

Dunn, W. (2008). A sensory-processing approach to supporting students with autism spectrum disorders. In R. L. Simpson & B. S. Myles (Eds.), *Educating children with autism: Strategies for effective practice* (pp. 299–356). Austin, TX: PRO-ED.

Durand, V. M., & Crimmins, D. (1992). *Motivation assessment scale (MAS).* Topeka, KS: Monaco.

Earles-Vollrath, T. L., Cook, K. T., Robbins, L., & Ben-Arieh, J. (2008). Instructional strategies to facilitate successful learning outcomes for students with autism spectrum disorders. In R. L. Simpson & B. S. Myles (Eds.), *Educating children and youth with autism—strategies for effective practice* (2nd ed.). Austin, TX: PRO-ED.

Faherty, C. (2000). *Asperger's . . . What does it mean to me? A workbook explaining self-awareness and life lessons to the child or youth with high functioning autism or Aspergers: Structured teaching for home and school.* Arlington, TX: Future Horizons.

Fighting Autism: Research, education, treatment. (n.d.). Retrieved March 19, 2008, from http://www.fightingautism.org/idea/autism.php

Fisher, C. (2006). Interventions in general education classrooms. In R. L. Koegel & L. K. Koegel (Eds.), *Pivotal response treatments for autism* (pp. 53–79). Maryland: Brooks.

Freeman, S., & Dake, L. (1997a). *Teach me language: A language manual for children with autism, Asperger's syndrome, and related developmental disorders.* Langley, BC: SKF Books.

Freeman, S., & Dake, L. (1997b). *The companion exercise forms for teach me Language: A language manual for children with autism, Asperger's Syndrome, and related developmental disorders.* Langley, BC: SKF Books.

Frost, L., & Bondy, A. (2002). *PECS: The Picture Exchange Communication System training manual* (2nd ed.). Cherry Hill, N.J.: Pyramid Educational Consultants.

Gagnon, E. (2001). *Power cards: Using special interests to motivate children and youth with Asperger syndrome and autism.* Shawnee Mission, KS: Autism Asperger.

Gerber, S. (2003). A developmental perspective on language assessment and intervention for children on the spectrum. *Topics in Language Disorders, 23*(2), 74–94.

Gilliam, J. E. (2006). *Gilliam Autism Rating Scale* (2nd ed.). Austin, TX: PRO-ED.

Goh, H. L., Iwata, B. A., & DeLeon, I. G. (2002). *Functional analysis screening tool (FAST).* Gainesville, FL: The Florida Center on Self-Injury.

Goldstein, H. (2002). Communication intervention for children with autism: A review of treatment efficacy. *Journal of Autism and Developmental Disorders, 32*(5), 373–396.

Grandin, T. (1995). *Thinking in pictures and other reports from my life with autism.* New York: Doubleday.

Grandin, T. (1996). *Thinking in pictures*. New York: Random House.

Gray, C. (1994a). *Comic strip conversations*. Arlington, TX: Future Horizons.

Gray, C. (1994b). *The new social story book*. Arlington, TX: Future Horizons.

Gray, C., & Garand, J. D. (1993). Social stories: Improving responses of students with autism with accurate social information. *Focus on Autistic Behavior, 8*(1), 1–10.

Greenspan, S. I., & Lewis, D. (2005). *The affect based language curriculum: An intensive program for families, therapists and teachers* (2nd ed.). Bethesda, MD: Interdisciplinary Council on Developmental and Learning Disorders (ICDL).

Greenspan, S. I., & Wieder, S. (2000). A developmental approach to difficulties in relating and communicating in autism spectrum disorders and related syndromes. In S. F. Warren & J. Reichle (Series Eds.) & A. M. Wetherby & B. M. Prizant (Vol. Eds.), *Communication and language intervention series Vol. 9. Autism spectrum disorders: A developmental transactional perspective* (pp. 279–306). Baltimore: Paul H. Brookes.

Gutstein, S., & Sheely, R. (2002a). *Relationship development intervention with children, adolescents, and adults: Social and emotional development activities for Asperger syndrome, autism*. London: Jessica Kingsley.

Gutstein, S. E., & Sheely, R. K. (2002b). *Relationship development intervention with young children: Social and emotional development activities for Asperger syndrome, autism, PDD, and NLD*. London: Jessica Kingsley.

Happe, F. G. E. (1991). Autobiographical writings. In U. Frith (Ed.), *Autism and Asperger syndrome* (pp. 207–242). London: Cambridge University Press.

Happe, F. G. E. (1994). An advanced test of theory of mind: Understanding of story characters' thoughts and feelings by able autistic, mentally handicapped, and normal children and adults, *Journal of Autism and Developmental Disorders, 24*(2), 129–154.

Howlin, P., Baron-Cohen, S., & Hadwin, J. (1999). *Teaching children with autism to mind-read: A practical guide*. West Sussex, UK: John Wiley & Sons.

Jackson, L. (2002). *Freaks, geeks and Asperger syndrome: A user guide to adolescence*. Philadelphia: Jessica Kingsley.

Janzen, J. E. (2003). *Understanding the nature of autism: A practical guide*. San Antonio, TX: Therapy Skill Builders.

Kanner, L. (1943). Autistic disturbances of affective contact. *Nervous Child, 2*, 217–250.

Kaplan, J. S., & Carter, J. (1995). *Beyond behavior modification: A cognitive-behavior approach to behavior management in the school* (3rd ed.). Austin, TX: PRO-ED.

Kashman, N., & Mora, J. (2005). *The sensory connection: An OT and SLP team approach* (Rev. ed.). Las Vegas, NV: Sensory Resources.

Klin, A., Carter, A., Volkmar, F. R., Cohen, D. J., Marans, W. D., & Sparrow, S. S. (1997). Assessment issues in children with autism. In D. J. Cohen & F. R. Volkmar (Eds.), *Handbook of autism and pervasive developmental disorders* (2nd ed., pp. 411–418). New York: John Wiley & Sons.

Koegel, R. L., Klein, E. F., Koegel, L. K., Boettcher, M. A., Brookman-Frazee, L., & Openden, D. (2006). Working with paraprofessionals to improve socialization in inclusive settings. In R. L. Koegel & L. K. Koegel (Eds.), *Pivotal response treatments for autism: Communication, social, & academic development* (pp. 189–198). Baltimore: Brookes.

Koegel, R. L., & Koegel, L. K. (2006). *Pivotal response treatments for autism*. Baltimore: Brookes.

Koegel, R., Schreffirnan, L., Good, A., Cerniglia, L., Murphy, C., & Koegel, L. K. (1989). *How to teach pivotal behaviors to children with autism: A training manual*. Santa Barbara: University of California. It can be downloaded at http://www.users.qwest.net/~tbharris/prt.htm

Krantz, P. J., & McClannahan, L. E. (1993). Teaching children with autism to initiate to peers: Effects of a script-fading procedure. *Journal of Applied Behavior Analysis, 26*, 121–132.

Krug, D., & Arick, J. (2003). *Asperger's disorder index* (KADI). Austin, TX: PRO-ED.

Leaf, R., & McEachin, J. (1999). *A work in progress: Behavior management strategies and a curriculum for intensive behavioral treatment of autism*. New York: DRL Books.

LoGiudice, C., & McConnell, N. (2004). *Room 28: A social language program*. East Moline, IL: LinguiSystems.

Lord, C., Rutter, M., DiLavore, P. C., & Risi, S. (2002). *The autism diagnostic observation schedule: Generic*. Los Angeles: Western Psychological Services.

Lord, C., Rutter, M., & Le Couteur, A. (1994). Autism diagnostic interview, revised: A revised version of a diagnostic interview for caregivers of individuals with possible pervasive developmental disorders. *Journal of Autism and Developmental Disorders, 24*, 659–685.

Maurice, C., Green, G., & Foxx, R. (2001). *Making a difference: Behavioral intervention for autism*. Austin, TX: PRO-ED.

Maurice, C., Green, G., & Luce, S. C. (Eds.). (1996). *Behavioral intervention for young children with autism: A manual for parents and professionals*. Austin, Texas: PRO-ED.

McAfee, J. (2002). *Navigating the social world: A curriculum for individuals with Asperger's syndrome, high functioning autism and related disorders*. Arlington, TX: Future Horizons.

McClannahan, L. E., & Krantz, P. J. (1999). Activity schedules for children with autism. Teaching independent behavior. In S. L. Harris (Series Ed.), *Topics in autism* (pp. 1–117). Bethesda, MD: Woodbine House.

Mesibov, G. B., Schopler, E., Schaffer, B., & Landrus, R. (1988). *Individualized assessment and treatment for autistic and developmentally disabled children: Adolescent and adult psychoeducational profile* (Vol. 4). Austin, TX: PRO-ED.

Miller-Kuhaneck, H., Henry, D. A., Glennon, T. J., & Mu, K. (2007). Development of the sensory processing measure-school: Initial studies of reliability and validity. *The American Journal of Occupational Therapy, 61*(2), 170–175.

Mirenda, P. (2003). Toward functional augmentative and alternative communication for students with autism: Manual signs, graphic symbols, and voice output communication aids. *Language, Speech, and Hearing Services in Schools, 34*, 203–216.

Morgan, J., & Shoop, S. A. (n.d.). USA Today: Lily Tomlin's "acts of love" help autism; Will raise funds for autism research. *Schafer Autism Report, 7*(214). Retrieved October 27, 2003, from http://www.usatoday.com/news/health/spotlighthealth/2003–10–17-tomlinautism_x.htm

Myles, B. S., Bock, S. J., & Simpson, R. L. (2000). *The Asperger Syndrome Diagnostic Scale*. Austin, TX: PRO-ED.

Myles, B. S., Cook, K. T., Miller, N. E., Rinner, L., & Robbins, L. A. (2000). *Asperger syndrome and sensory issues: Practical solutions for making sense of the world*. Shawnee Mission, KS: Autism Asperger.

Myles, S. B., Trautman, L. M., & Schelvan, L. R. (2004). *The hidden curriculum: Practical solutions for understanding unstated rules in social situations*. Shawnee Mission, KS: Autism Asperger.

National Institutes of Health (NIH) News. (2004, October 12). *NIMH grant to explore genetics of autism*. Retrieved November 22, 2007, from http://www.nih.gov/news/pr/oct2004/nimh-12a.htm

National Research Council. (2001). *Educating children with autism*. Committee on Educational Interventions for Children With Autism. Division of Behavioral and Social Sciences and Education. Washington, DC: National Academy Press.

Ogle, D. (1986). K-W-L: A teaching model that develops active reading of expository text. *The Reading Teacher, 39*, 564–570.

Ogletree, B., & Oren, T. (1998). Structured yet functional: An alternative conceptualization of treatment for communication impairment in autism. *Focus on Autism and Other Developmental Disabilities, 13*(4), 228–233.

Packer, J. A. (1997). *How rude! The teenagers' guide to good manners, proper behavior, and not grossing people out*. Minneapolis, MN: Free Spirit.

Parham, L. D., Ecker, C., Miller-Kuhaneck, H., Henry, D. A., & Glennon, T. J. (2007). *Sensory processing measure (SPM) manual*. Los Angeles: Western Psychological Services.

Partington, W. J. (2006). *The assessment of basic language and learning skills-R (ABLLS-R)*. Pleasant Hill, CA: Behavior Analysts.

Phelps-Terasaki, D., & Phelps-Gunn, T. (2007). *Test of pragmatic language*. Austin, TX: PRO-ED.

Prelock, P. A., Beatson, J., Bitner, B., Broder, C., & Ducker, A. (2003). Interdisciplinary assessment of young children with autism spectrum disorders. *Language Speech and Hearing Services in Schools, 34*, 194–202.

Prizant, B. M., Wetherby, A. M., & Rydell, P. J. (2000). Communication intervention issues for children with autism spectrum disorders. In S. F. Warren & J. R. Reichle (Series Eds.) & A. M. Wetherby & B. M. Prizant (Vol. Eds.), *Communication and language intervention series: Vol. 9. Autism spectrum disorders: A transactional developmental perspective* (pp. 193–224). Baltimore: Paul H. Brookes.

Quill, K. A. (2000). *Do watch listen say: Social and communication intervention for children with autism.* Baltimore: Paul H. Brooke.

Reese, P. B., & Challenner, N. C. (1999). *Autism and PDD social skills lessons series.* East Moline, IL: LinguiSystems.

Reynolds, C. R., & Kamphaus, R. W. (1992). *Behavior assessment system for children—manual* (2nd ed.). Circle Pines, MN: American Guidance Service.

Reynolds, C. R., & Kamphaus, R. W. (2004). *Manual for the behavior assessment system for children* (2nd ed.). Circle Pines, MN: American Guidance Service.

Roid, G. H. (2005). *Stanford-Binet intelligence scales* (5th ed.). Rolling Meadows, IL: Riverside.

Rutter, M., Le Couteur, A., & Lord, C. (2003). *The autism diagnostic interview-revised* (ADI-R). Los Angeles, CA: Western Psychological Services.

Sansosti, F., & Powell-Smith, K. (2008). Using computer-presented stories and video models to increase the social communication skills of children with high-functioning autism spectrum disorders. *Journal of Positive Behavior Interventions, 10*(3), 162–178.

Schopler, E., Lansing, M. D., Reichler, R. J., & Marcus, L. M. (2005). *PEP-3: Psychoeducational profile (3rd ed.): TEACCH individualized psychoeducational assessment for children with autism spectrum disorders.* Austin, TX: PRO-ED.

Schopler, E., Reichler, R., & Renner, B. R. (1988). *The childhood autism rating scale* (CARS). Los Angeles: Western Psychological Services.

Semel, E., Wiig, E., & Secord, W. (2003). *Clinical evaluation of language fundamentals* (4th ed.) (CELF-4). San Antonio, TX: Harcourt Assessment.

Sigafoos, J., O'Reilly, M., & de la Cruz, B. (2007). *How to use video modeling and video prompting.* Austin TX: PRO-ED.

Sigman, M., Ruskin, E., Arbelle, S., Corona, R., Dissanayake, C., Espinosa, M., et al. (1999). Social competence in children with autism, Down syndrome, and other developmental delays: A longitudinal study. *Monographs of the Society for Research in Child Development, 64*(1), 1–114.

Simpson, R. L., de Boer-Ott, S. R., & Myles, B. S. (2003). Inclusion of learners with autism spectrum disorders in general education settings. *Topics in Language Disorders, 23*(2), 116–133.

Simpson, R. L., Myles, B. S., & LaCava, P. G. (2008). Understanding and responding to the needs of children and youth with autism spectrum disorders. In R. L. Simpson & B. S. Myles (Eds.), *Educating children with autism—strategies for effective practice* (pp. 1–59). Austin, TX: PRO-ED.

Snyder-McLean, L. K., Solomonson, B., McLean, J. E., & Sack, S. (1984). Structuring joint action routines: A strategy for facilitating communication and language development in the classroom. *Seminars in Speech and Language, 5,* 213–228.

Sparrow, S. S., Cicchetti, D. V., & Balla, D. A. (2005). *Vineland adaptive behavior scales* (2nd ed.). Circle Pines, MN: America Guidance Service.

Sugai, G., Horner, R., Dunlap, G., Heineman, M., Lewis, T., Nelson, et al. (2000). Applying positive behavior support and functional behavioral assessment in schools. *Journal of Positive Behavior Interventions, 2*(3), 131–143.

Sundberg, M., & Partington, J. (1998). *Teaching language to children with autism or other developmental disabilities.* Pleasant Hill, CA: Behavior Analysts.

Sussman, F. (1999). *More than words: Helping parents promote communication and social skills in children with autism spectrum disorders.* Toronto, Ontario: The Hanen Centre.

Sussman, F. (2006). *Talk ability: People skills for verbal children on the autism spectrum—A guide for parents.* Toronto, Ontario: The Hanen Centre.

Swaggart, B. L., Gagnon, E., Bock, S. J., Earles, T. L., Quinn, C., Myles, B. S., et al. (1995). Using social stories to teach social and behavioral skills to children with autism. *Focus on Autistic Behavior, 10*(1), 1–15.

Tager-Flusberg, H. (1997). Perspectives on language and communication in autism. In D. J. Cohen & F. R. Volkmar (Eds.), *Handbook of autism and pervasive developmental disorders* (2nd ed., pp. 894–900). New York: John Wiley & Sons.

Toomey, M. (2002). The language of perspective taking. Marblehead, MA: Circuit Publications.

Wechsler, D. (1997). *Wechsler adult intelligence scale* (3rd ed.). San Antonio, TX: Psychological Corp.

Wechsler, D. (2002). *Wechsler preschool and primary scale of intelligence* (3rd ed.). San Antonio, TX: Psychological Corp.

Wechsler, D. (2003). *Wechsler intelligence scale for children* (4th ed.). San Antonio, TX: Psychological Corp.

Wetherby, A., & Prizant, B. (1989). The expression of communicative intent: Assessment guidelines. *Seminars in Speech and Language, 10*(1), 77–91.

Wetherby, A. M., Prizant, B. M., & Schuler, A. L. (2000). Understanding the nature of communication and language impairments. In S. F. Warren & J. R. Reichle (Series Eds.) & A. M. Wetherby & B. M. Prizant (Vol. Eds.), *Communication and language intervention series: Vol. 9. Autism spectrum disorders: A transactional developmental perspective* (pp. 109–141). Baltimore: Paul H. Brookes.

Williams, D. (1995). *Somebody somewhere: Breaking free from the world of autism.* Ontario, Canada: Doubleday.

Wilson, C. C. (1993). *Room 14: A social language program.* East Moline, IL: LinguiSystems.

Wing, L., & Gould, J. (1979). Severe impairments of social interaction and associated abnormalities in children: Epidemiology and classification. *Journal of Autism and Childhood Schizophrenia, 9*(1), 11–29.

Winner, M. G. (2002). *Thinking about you thinking about me philosophy and strategies to further develop perspective taking and communicative abilities for persons with social cognitive deficits: Asperger syndrome, pervasive developmental disorder-not otherwise specified (PDD-NOS), high-functioning autism, attention deficit hyperactive disorder (ADHD), hyperlexia, nonverbal learning disability (NVLD).* San Jose, CA: Author.

Wood, M. M., Davis, K. R., Swindle, F. L., & Quirk, C. (1996). *Developmental therapy—developmental teaching: Fostering social-emotional competence in troubled children and youth* (3rd ed.). Austin, TX: PRO-ED.

Woodcock, W. R., McGrew, S. K., & Mather, N. (2001). *Woodcock-Johnson III tests of achievement.* Rolling Meadows, IL: Riverside.

Woods, J. J., & Wetherby, A. M. (2003). Early identification of and intervention for infants and toddlers who are at risk for autism spectrum disorder. *Language, Speech, and Hearing Services in Schools, 34,* 180–193.

Index

CORWIN

A SAGE Company

The Corwin logo—a raven striding across an open book—represents the union of courage and learning. Corwin is committed to improving education for all learners by publishing books and other professional development resources for those serving the field of PreK–12 education. By providing practical, hands-on materials, Corwin continues to carry out the promise of its motto: **"Helping Educators Do Their Work Better."**

CPSIA information can be obtained
at www.ICGtesting.com
Printed in the USA
FSOW03n1831151214
3918FS

9 781412 957762